TRAIL GUIDE TO THE SCRIPTURES

TRAIL GUIDE TO THE SCRIPTURES

1 PETER

SHANE L. BISHOP

invite
PRESS
Plano, Texas

CONTENTS

• • • • • • • • • • • • •

WELCOME TO THE TRAIL

I have always loved outdoor hiking, especially in the Great Smoky Mountains. In our younger days, my wife Melissa and I would set out from a trailhead for a day-hike to "see what we saw." Every vista, surging waterfall, and black bear sighting was exciting! But after a few years, we had hiked many of the trails so often that some of the luster had diminished. Even in the most beautiful of places, what is predictable can become invisible.

Then we discovered the transforming power of a guidebook as a trail companion. Familiar trails suddenly became unexplored as the mountains suddenly offered both scars and hints of previous lives. These clues told the stories of vanished people and cultures who have long since disappeared. They offer testimony both to devastating forest fires and clear cutting and to the healing and restorative power of God's creation.

Our times in the mountains have become richer and more rewarding because we know something of the forgotten people who have walked these trails, played in these streams, and worked these fields before us. Hearing their stories, singing their songs, and walking into their remaining cabins and churches enrich us and flood our imaginations.

The Bible is very much like a mountain trail. You can simply read it, and the Holy Spirit will speak if your heart is open. But after a while, reading the same material over and over from the same point of view can fail to engage us. We know we "should" read the Bible, but all too often it becomes a dutiful chore rather than a faith adventure.

Might I be so bold as to request the honor of being your trail guide? Allow me to walk alongside you as you encounter God's Word and share the experience of four decades of preaching, academic study, historical research, and my time in the land of the Bible. Let me show you some magnificent views and open a world before you that you only suspected to have existed at all.

Welcome to the Bible!

My goal in writing is to produce a verse-by-verse trek through entire books of the Bible that you can't put down. I hope the narrative that sprawls before you will "sizzle and pop" for both the novice and experienced Bible reader. I hope to sweep you up in the story, tell a few stories of my own, offer some lessons for living, and relay the author's intent. I will treat each book as a single unit and respect the fact that biblical authors wrote "the way they wrote" and "what they wrote" for a reason. There will not be a lot of cross-referencing or attempts to "soften" the implications of the message. I will include what the authors chose to include and exclude what they chose to exclude.

We will faithfully walk the trail in front of us and do so until we come to the end.

We will then walk another trail through another book of the Bible.

That is how these Trail Guides work.

I pray that when we have completed our journey, not only will you better understand the material, but you will better know yourself and have strengthened your connection with Jesus Christ.

Are you ready? I am. Let's go!

TRAILHEAD: 1 PETER

Every adventure worth taking involves risk. When we read the Bible, we dare to believe that God, the creator of everything, will speak to us. The risk associated with God is that he will change our entire world. By drawing us closer to Jesus Christ, we risk relationships, profession, hobbies, and our identity.

However, every adventure worth taking involves substantial reward. As we open our hearts to the word of God, we allow ourselves to accept love, peace, and joy. We begin to see the world through fresh eyes because our perspective shifts. It's in these moments we realize what used to be scary is now exhilarating.

Trail Guide to the Scriptures: 1 Peter is an adventure worth the risk. Rev. Shane Bishop will guide you along the well-worn trail of the Apostle Peter. The trail of Peter presents many challenges, but with the direction of your trail guide, you will be able to withstand and even appreciate the tests. As you navigate 1 Peter, write your thoughts on the events in each chapter and how the Scripture affects you. Answer the questions that are presented with honesty and sincerity and copy or memorize your favorite verses. The goal of any journey is not simply to finish but to be changed along the way.

Also, I would recommend traveling this journey with someone else. Peter did not serve or evangelize alone, and neither should we. Invite a friend, co-worker, family member, or spouse and make memories together. Discuss the scenery as you traverse the book of 1 Peter, and you will be surprised that your viewpoint is unique compared to that of your traveling companion.

Finally, open your heart to the word of God and the experience of Rev. Shane. If you do, you will not end this adventure the same way you began. In the words of Peter, you will face many trials, but if you endure them, your faith will be proven genuine. Welcome to the trail.

Kevin Siddle, Director of Adult Education,
Christ Church, Fairview Heights, Illinois

1 PETER
TRAIL INSTRUCTIONS

The first task when approaching any book of the Bible is to place it in a historical context. Apart from this, we are tempted to think the Bible happened "once upon a time, in a place far away," rather than embrace the reality the Bible happened in "real time in places our feet can still touch the ground." When it comes to ancient literature, there are usually multiple options concerning this task. In the end, you do your research, make your best guess, and "pick a side and play."

I believe 1 Peter was written just before his martyrdom in 64 AD and a couple of years before the Jewish Revolt in 66 AD. I will work from this assumption knowing that if I am wrong, I am not wrong by much. With this context in mind, we are reminded that on July 19, 64 AD, two-thirds of the city Rome burned to the ground. The fire raged for six days, then reignited and burned for another three days. The emperor, Nero, probably burned the city down himself because he wanted to rebuild it and could never have gained the political support he needed to do so. With Rome still smoldering and rumors flying, Nero needed a scapegoat to divert attention from the fact that he had motive and the fire did not touch any of his property.

Enter the Christians. This fledgling movement had come out of Israel and quickly splintered from Judaism. It centered upon the life, teachings, and resurrection of a Jew named Jesus of Nazareth whom the Roman governor Pontius Pilate had crucified in Jerusalem. The central claim was that Jesus of Nazareth had risen from the dead, and there were plenty of eyewitnesses. His disciples, led by Peter and John and emerging leaders such as the Apostle Paul, had started a sect within Judaism that developed a theology too distinct to be Jewish and too potent to be contained. Its adherents claimed the movement to be fueled by an irresistible force they called the Holy Spirit. Though burgeoning, Christianity was unpopular, even scandalized, by those not adhering to it. As Christianity separated itself from Judaism, it forfeited specific legal protections that the Romans had exclusively offered the Jews. From the Roman point of view, Christians refused to worship the emperor, refused to pledge ultimate allegiance to the empire, wouldn't worship Roman gods, and served as a clear and present danger to the lucrative industry that artfully produced idols. Christians were bad for business and bad for morale, and that made them vulnerable. It was the perfect storm.

Persecution of Christians soon spread from Rome and varied from contained and sporadic to relentless and sadistic. It was widely reported that Nero rolled Christians in pitch and used them in his garden as torches. In addition, extremely out-of-favor Christians in the Roman Colosseum were exposed to wild, starving animals for public entertainment. To most Romans, Christianity looked a lot like Judaism, except they seemed more enigmatic and were annoyingly evangelistic. Christian practice was rumored to be most strange, even sinister. They ate and drank the body and blood of their martyred leader, denied the existence of the gods, were accused of splitting up families, met secretly in homes, and proclaimed the imminent return of Jesus of Nazareth, whom they now called Christ. The Christian canvas was a perfect fit for Nero's frame.

While Jewish Christians had been enduring anti-Semitic persecution for three decades, it was a new and painful experience for the Gentile Christians and one for which they were unequipped. As fear threatened the Christian movement, Peter wrote this general letter of encouragement to be circulated among the Christians of Asia Minor. His intent was to offer perspective and hope during increasingly anxious times. The big idea was, "Here is how Christians act when times get tough. Here is how to behave in such a way that even the worst slanders Satan has to offer won't stick." Peter's love for the people to whom he writes is undeniable, and his heart breaks for the pain they are enduring and about to endure. You get the sense that Peter wishes he had better news. He realizes that being a Jesus follower will require increasingly greater levels of sacrifice from those claiming his name.

I PETER
TRAIL RATING

●●●●●●●●●●●●●●●●●●

LENGTH: SHORT
DIFFICULTY: MODERATE

Some years ago, I was hiking the Chimney Tops trail in the Great Smoky Mountains. It is a popular trail because it is not very long and the views are spectacular. It is however, steep and ascends 1,400 feet in two miles. The footing is often wet and always uneven. If you don't pay attention you will stumble and fall. There is nothing good going to happen if you do. There are no snack cafes, rest areas or first aid stops. If you are not an avid hiker, there are a few places where your legs are burning to the point you feel like they are on fire, your lungs feel like they are going to explode and you are sure you cannot walk another step. That is what I hear anyway.

On this particular morning, I noticed a young woman pushing the kind of baby buggy (you take to the mall) at the trailhead just ahead of us. She was dressed like she had just left church and had on dress shoes with heels. I thought, "Lady, this isn't going to go well for you." It didn't. She should have checked the trail rating before she started. She needed a two hundred yard trail that was paved and perfectly flat. She didn't even make it fifty yards before she turned back. Having some idea of the difficulty of a trail is helpful if you are walking up a mountain. It is also helpful if you are trekking through a book of the Bible.

I would rate I Peter as a moderate trail. It is relatively short and not too steep. That being said, it isn't a leisurely stroll either. If you are a beginner, I Peter is not a bad place to start. If you have been hiking your whole life, there will be plenty to engage you. There are some challenging places and anytime you are in the mountains there is danger.

This is an excellent place to begin this Trail Guide to the Scriptures series. But don't wear your church shoes.

Signposts to guide you.

 INTRO   **LISTS**

 CHAPTERS   **QUESTIONS**

 FACTS   **WHERE YOU ARE**

Getting Our Bearings

● ●

> This letter is from Peter, an apostle of Jesus Christ.
> I am writing to God's chosen people who are living
> as foreigners in the provinces of Pontus, Galatia,
> Cappadocia, Asia, and Bithynia. (1 Peter 1:1)

This letter was written by the fisherman Peter who was the leader of the original twelve disciples of Jesus Christ. Jesus had once declared that Peter was a rock. He even changed his name from Simon to Peter. It took a while, but Peter finally lived into that name. In tough times you need a rock for a leader. He writes some three decades after the resurrection. The letter was probably dictated from Peter to Silas, who put pen to parchment in far better Greek than a Galilean like Peter would have been able to produce. This letter clearly says it is from "Peter, an apostle of Jesus Christ," and there is no reason to think that it isn't.

Peter writes to Christians in the far northeastern part of the Roman Empire. Despite being in relatively close proximity to Israel, the text suggests that the audience was more Gentile (non-Jewish) than Jewish. My assumption is that the churches in this region were planted when Spirit-filled Jews who were in Jerusalem at Pentecost returned home filled with the Holy Spirit! The movement quickly spilled from the synagogues into the Gentile populations and surged from there.

1

In a few years, both the congregations and the driving local leadership shifted from predominantly Jewish to overwhelmingly Gentile. These increasingly heterogeneous churches had something in common other than proximity: persecution.

> God the Father knew you and chose you long ago, and his Spirit has made you holy. As a result, you have obeyed him and have been cleansed by the blood of Jesus Christ. (1 Peter 1:2)

Peter is doing something bodacious. Perhaps even outrageous. He is claiming for all Christians what the Old Testament promises to the Jews.

Judaism began when God unilaterally approached a man named Abram (later Abraham) and promised him . . . everything. The Jews were a holy (set apart for a special purpose) people and God's very own possession. Jews in this time period took pride in their special relationship with God and would have daily thanked God that they were not born Gentiles. The covenant between Yahweh (Hebrew for God) and his people was established in written Law and had been consecrated through ritual animal sacrifice. Now a new narrative emerged. Christians became the new Jews. Non-believing Jews became the new Gentiles. Suddenly, faith in the work of Christ became more consequential in determining "God's people" than being racially Jewish. Faith in Christ became more consequential than following the Law of Moses. The shift was cataclysmic.

> All praise to God, the Father of our Lord Jesus Christ. It is by his great mercy that we have been born again, because God raised Jesus Christ from the dead. (1 Peter 1:3a)

Peter seems so overwhelmed by his own claim that he stops the narrative and offers a short doxology (praise to God)! The preacher is giving himself an "amen!" God is not addressed as "the God of Abraham, Isaac, and Jacob," but rather, God is the "Father of our Lord Jesus Christ." How did we Gentiles get dealt into salvation history? God's love and mercy. When Jesus rose from the dead, it changed everything. Even the Sabbath Day for Christians shifted from Saturday to Sunday! The central event of Christianity is the literal resurrection of Jesus Christ from the dead. It is what separates us from every other religion.

> Now we live with great expectation, and we have a priceless inheritance—an inheritance that is kept in heaven for you, pure and undefiled, beyond the reach of change and decay. (1 Peter 1:3b–4)

Because of the resurrection, death, the ultimate human enemy and inescapable punishment of a fallen humanity, gets its proverbial butt kicked. The cessation of human life now shifts from the end to the beginning. Before the resurrection our reward for faithfulness seemingly came in time and space. Earthly life was all the eternity you got, and you "couldn't take it with you." Post resurrection, our primary reward comes in the afterlife, leaving earthly life a blip in an infinite reality. Undefiled treasures are preserved for us in heaven. This is something of which Jesus directly spoke.

The Greek word translated "inheritance" is the same concept used to describe the Promised Land in the Old Testament. Moses didn't just lead the Hebrew children out from Egyptian slavery; he led them into God's will for them. The Promised Land was not a concept to be grasped but an inheritance to be possessed. Peter instructs us that the Christian endgame is found not in the limited geography and resources of Israel but in the limitless space and wealth of eternity. This expansive shift was anticipated in the very heart of the promise that Abraham would "bring blessing to the earth" and in the conclusion of the twenty-third Psalm, "I will dwell in the house of the Lord forever" (Psalm 23:6, NIV). Peter is arguing that the emergence of Christianity is the fulfillment of a promise going back to the origins of monotheistic (one God) belief itself.

> And through your faith, God is protecting you by his power until you receive this salvation, which is ready to be revealed on the last day for all to see. (1 Peter 1:5)

Faith is the substance of the things for which we hope (Hebrews 11:1). It is a firm belief in what we cannot yet substantiate. A capacity for faith is what God saw in Abraham, and without faith it is "impossible to please God" (Hebrews 11:6). The idea is this: "What Jesus did then changes things now, and soon everyone will see it."

The Greek word translated "protect" is a military word denoting the kind of protection a fort outpost offers those on the outskirts of a civilization. God will protect our souls as we endure persecution and struggle with our frailties in exposed territories. God will win the war, but God is with us on the borders and in the battles until that victory is consummated. "Nero may destroy our bodies, but God protects our souls!" Finally, there is an element of vindication. Those who hold to the faith in difficult times will see salvation, and in the fullness of time, others will see that salvation as well. This brings to mind the vindication portion of the twenty-third Psalm that declares,

"You prepare a table before me in the presence of my enemies" (Psalm 23:5, NIV).

> So be truly glad. There is wonderful joy ahead, even though you must endure many trials for a little while. These trials will show that your faith is genuine. It is being tested as fire tests and purifies gold—though your faith is far more precious than mere gold. (1 Peter 1:6–7a)

Why Be Glad When Trials Come?

Joy awaits us on the other side.

Trials last only for a season.

Faithfulness in trials testifies to our faith. Trials purify our faith. Mountain hiking has taught me something about endurance. I have pushed up many mountain trails when my legs and my lungs were on fire in the hope of finishing what I started (and the fear of emasculation since my wife, Melissa, is always ahead of me). Peter pushes it further. Not only are the treacherous stretches of trail navigable and survivable, but we are better for having traversed them! Just as fire refines gold, persecution and hardship expose and refine those parts of us not resembling Christ and transform us ever more into the image of our creator.

> So when your faith remains strong through many trials, it will bring you much praise and glory and honor on the day when Jesus Christ is revealed to the whole world. (1 Peter 1:7b)

One day when I was in my mid-twenties, I came home from work and noticed that something in the house was different. After a quick inspection, I noticed that all of my trophies from high school and college were gone. They had been lovingly displayed on a shelving unit (by me), and now they were gone. This was back when you actually had to win something to get a trophy, so I liked them a great deal. They said to me each day, "Shane, you are awesome!" When I inquired as to their whereabouts, Melissa said glibly, "I threw them in the trash, and they are gone. You are a grown man. Grown men don't need trophies." Wrong! Clearly, she didn't know me at all, but what are you going to do? The promise offered is that when Jesus wins it all, Jesus will personally hand out the trophies, and they won't be made of plastic and wood.

Remember that the author of 1 Peter is among the most manic of all New Testament characters. No one gets it "more right" and no one gets it "more wrong" than Peter, and it can all happen in three seconds. It was Peter who declared Jesus to be the son of God and Peter who denied Jesus in the courtyard. That same Peter who choked under pressure in the high priest's courtyard became the kind of man who could lead others in how to navigate and be faithful in times of persecution, and that is miraculous.

It makes me think that God can use anyone. Perhaps even you and me!

 ## Questions for Discussion and Reflection

1. Are you in a period of life where your faith is easily understood and thing are going well, or are you in the process of navigating a sudden change?

2. Have you experienced the joy that awaits us on the other side of a trial? How did the trial begin, and how are you better for it?

Prophets, Angels, and Edmund

C. S. Lewis' *The Chronicles of Narnia* were a big part of my childhood. Looking back, not only did these books entertain me and open up the world of reading, but they taught me about myself and about God. I was shocked in seminary to discover how impactful C. S. Lewis had been on my foundational theology. It is an ever-present reminder of how important faith development is in children. In *The Lion, the Witch, and the Wardrobe*, the great lion Aslan willingly sacrifices himself at the hands of the evil White Witch to save a particularly wicked boy named Edmund. Edmund is so selfish that he would do anything or sell out anyone just to get more Turkish Delight candy from the Witch. The damage Edmund causes those who love him most is incalculable.

As the book unfolded, I found myself not having much pity for Edmund. Why would the noble, strong, and perfect Aslan die for the salvation of a stupid, careless little boy who seemed devoid of human virtue? I found myself rooting against Edmund and wishing he, instead of more honorable creatures, would be turned to stone by the White Witch. My sense of justice was heightened. Why should Edmund get better than he deserves when his actions caused others to get far

7

worse than they deserve? In fact, it seemed the only one really rooting for the salvation of Edmund was Aslan himself. Aslan seemed determined that Edmund would not get what he deserved and left us all wondering why. I asked myself over and over again, "What is wrong with Aslan?" In Narnia, as it is in our world, the best one we ever had gave his life for the worst one of all. Nothing could be more unfair. And then one day it hit me. If you can save the worst, you can save the rest. If Edmund could not be saved, no one else could have been saved either. It is here that we get to the heart of the matter: I root against Edmund because I am he. I am the one who did not deserve the salvation Christ died to bring. I am the one who has caused pain to others. Edmund, you stupid, careless, selfish little boy! I am Edmund. And so are you.

> You love him even though you have never seen him. Though you do not see him now, you trust him; and you rejoice with a glorious, inexpressible joy. The reward for trusting him will be the salvation of your souls. (1 Peter 1:8–9)

One thing Peter always had going for him as a leader in the early church was that he personally knew Jesus. Not only did he know Jesus, but Jesus chose him as the team captain of the disciples. It gave Peter a gravitas with which not even Paul could compete. Rather than use this reality to elevate himself above his readers, Peter chooses another path entirely. He applauds the astounding faith required of those who had never seen Jesus in the flesh but loved him regardless. He turns their disadvantage into an advantage by turning his advantage into a disadvantage. It was a sacrificial act of leadership. It was also brilliant.

As we move from the Gospels to the rest of the New Testament, we realize that we are increasingly dealing with people who had never seen or personally known Jesus of Nazareth. They did not know what he looked like, never heard him teach, never witnessed a miracle, and never laid eyes on him after the resurrection. What the first Christians accepted by sight, subsequent Christians would have to accept on faith. Peter's church consisted of people who lived a generation after Jesus ascended. Their knowledge of Jesus came through the witness of the apostles and Scripture. They grew to love and trust a savior they had not seen. We define belief in what you have not seen as "faith." Of all the attributes that God most values in a human being, faith is at the top of the list. The Bible teaches that faith is rewarded in two distinct dimensions, on earth and in heaven. Concerning our earthly lives, we are assured that faith produces a type of joy that is indescribable. In this sense joy is a by-product of a life aligned with Jesus and should not be confused with happiness, which is a temporary response to favorable circumstances. Faith produces a joy that is not only perpetual but straight-up glorious. In the Bible "glory" isn't just an abstraction, but it is something you can see. In this sense Christians "wear" or "put on" joy as we would wear a coat, and the coat looks great on us!

Salvation is the ultimate reward of faith. It is the endgame of faith. It is that which faith believes. For those waiting for a savior, the arrival of Jesus in Bethlehem was their salvation. For those awaiting the Second Coming, Jesus' arrival will be their salvation. For those awaiting heaven, the cessation of human life will be their salvation. The Greek word translated "salvation" is connected with four closely related concepts:

deliverance from danger, healing from disease, pardon from condemnation, and the victory over the power of sin. Faith in Jesus Christ is the key to both temporal and eternal life. This salvation must begin in time and space, but it plays out in the eternity of heaven.

> This salvation was something even the prophets wanted to know more about when they prophesied about this gracious salvation prepared for you. They wondered what time or situation the Spirit of Christ within them was talking about when he told them in advance about Christ's suffering and his great glory afterward. They were told that their messages were not for themselves, but for you. (1 Peter 1:10–12a)

The Bible was written by human beings who each brought their own experience and perspectives to the table, but it was inspired by the Holy Spirit. We don't believe God personally wrote the Bible like God wrote the Ten Commandments on two stone tablets, but we believe that God wrote the Bible through people. That is why we say that the Bible is "the Word of God." To support this way of thinking, Peter sometimes seems surprised by his own wisdom and insight. Peter suggests the same thing must have happened to the prophets. This passage points to the human curiosity a prophet has concerning what the Holy Spirit is saying through him. This points to the source of true prophecy as rooted in God's Word.

There is a "double ring" to Old Testament prophecy. It applies to the spiritual and political context of the prophet, and it applies to that which lies beyond it. Peter claims that the prophets themselves sensed this double ring and that Old Testament prophecy both points toward and anticipates Christ.

When God speaks through what we say, write, or post, we often do not know the full extent of the impact because we lack the bandwidth to see the big picture. It is important to know that the prophets had the same limitations we do, but they were faithful to speak what God prompted them to say nonetheless. God not only spoke but still speaks to us through the prophets. That is why the Old Testament still matters.

> And now this Good News has been announced to you by those who preached in the power of the Holy Spirit sent from heaven. (1 Peter 1:12b)

When I would read *The Chronicles of Narnia* series as a child, I always wondered how the plots of the individual books were going to end but equally wondered how the overarching story of the series proper would be resolved. In a very real sense, the "small 's' stories" linked the reader into the "big 'S' Story." We should read the Bible in the same way. Peter reminds us that the Good News of Christ was first anticipated by prophets under the influence of the Holy Spirit. Spirit-filled preaching—past, present, and future—not only continues the conversation but is the supernatural gift of God to the church.

> It is all so wonderful that even the angels are eagerly watching these things happen. (1 Peter 1:12c)

Once again Peter seems overwhelmed by what the Spirit has written through him. He gets done and thinks, "Wow! This is awesome! I could never have come up with any of this on my own!" Have you ever had an opportunity to publicly share or privately speak into someone's life, and it was clear that God was speaking through you? In that moment you knew more than you know, you spoke more clearly than you can speak, and you were giving more than you had? In those moments we are simply conduits from a God who has something to say to a person that they need to hear. And when that presentation or conversation is concluded, there is a sense of palpable awe. "The God of creation, the God of Abraham, Isaac, and Jacob, the God who raised Christ Jesus from the dead, actually spoke through me!" Wow! How awesome is that? The angels were hanging on every word!

Three years ago Melissa was speaking to a group of women, and I listened to the Facebook Live broadcast. Melissa has a spiritual brilliance about her that I get to experience every day, but she is never rushing to accept invitations to speak. I tell people that she is like a Hollywood actress who hardly makes movies, but when she makes them, they are incredible. That night God spoke some profound things through her, and I couldn't wait to discuss them when she got home. When she walked through the door, I hit her with a quote before she could even set her purse down. She looked at me blankly and said, "That is awesome. Who said that?" "You did! Tonight," I said. She paused for a moment and simply replied, "Wow."

Peter grew up in Galilee. He had the kind of personality that would make him the kind of guy who "knew everyone." He was a commercial fisherman by trade who seemed to be running a very common template for his life. There is no reason whatsoever that history should remember Simon Peter except that God got ahold of him. A disciple first of John the Baptist and then of Jesus, Peter took his natural leadership gifts and leveraged them for the kingdom. And yet I am sure there were those who simply didn't buy into this blustery man they went to elementary school with. They were no doubt quick to remember every stupid thing he had ever said and every selfish thing he had ever done. People are quick to see the Edmund in all of us. Yet because of Christ, Peter matured from a man suffering a bad case of "foot-in-mouth disease" to a steady, respected, and trusted leader of God's people. And sometimes God spoke things through Peter in undeniable ways that surprised even him. Those words still reverberate to this day.

Sometimes God speaks through the likes of people like us too.

Wow!

Questions for Discussion and Reflection

1. Would others be able to "see" the faith, joy, and salvation you have in Christ by the way you act?

2. Have you ever had an opportunity to publicly share or privately speak into someone's life and it was clear God was speaking through you?

The Endgame

To navigate, you have to know where you are, know where you want to be, and have some clarity concerning how to get from "here to there." Peter has opened this letter celebrating the hope we have in Christ that leads to eternal life. Eternity is where his audience is headed. For many, they will arrive early. They are living under an ever-increasing persecution that is going to get worse and not better. In the text we are about to explore, Peter offers some navigation tools to help them and us move from "here to there" in challenging times.

I remember when I made the DuQuoin High School freshman football team. Back in those days, there was no football in southern Illinois other than high school ball, so not one of us had previously played a single down of organized football. It was exciting to be a football player, to receive my black helmet, an assortment of pads I had no idea what to do with, and my practice uniform. All I could think about was how awesome it was going to be to play under the lights, celebrate wins, ride in a pickup truck in the homecoming parade down Main Street, and see my name in the team listing. But I soon discovered that it was something else entirely to endure two-hour, two per day practices in the blistering August heat, get pummeled by upperclassmen, run until the world turned purple and be-

gan to spin clockwise, and undergo freshman initiation ritu-
als that would now be illegal in all fifty states and parts of
Canada. I might also note that I played in an era in which
it was commonly thought that dehydration produced character in young men, and to aid the process, they fed us salt
pills that we swallowed up like racehorses. It was something
else entirely to pass out into my pillow after every practice,
get out of bed too stiff to move, have contusions all over
my body, and walk a mile to the high school to put on my
soured equipment from the drying room that smelled like
the business side of a yak.

The idea of being a football player was a romantic one.
The reality of conforming my life to that of a football player
played out in blood, sweat, and tears. By the time I was
a senior, they had changed my number to 25. I still have
the red mesh game jersey I wore on Senior Night with my
name sewn on the back hanging in my closet. A while back
I decided to try it on, and I couldn't believe it still fit! Then
I remembered that I wore that jersey with a huge pair of
shoulder pads underneath it.

As Christianity spread across the northeastern part of
the Roman Empire in the second half of the first century,
hundreds of new converts were being made by the day. Join-
ing the Jesus team was countercultural, edgy, and exciting,
but it was increasingly evident that living a Christian ethic
under the systematic persecution of the emperor Nero was
going to be a different thing entirely. Jesus never downplayed
the cost of discipleship. He said over and over, *"If you want
to follow me, it is going to be really hard."* Peter was taught
discipleship by Jesus himself. He had seen the best of it, the

worst of it, and the best of it again. In light of the challenges Christians faced in the roaring 60s AD on one hand and the anticipated eternal salvation coming on the other, Peter offers some gritty navigation tools for tough times.

 ## Questions for Discussion and Reflection

1. Do you find it challenging to be a Christian today? If so, how?

Gritty Navigational Tools for Tough Times

So prepare your minds for action and exercise self-control. Put all your hope in the gracious salvation that will come to you when Jesus Christ is revealed to the world. (1 Peter 1:13)

Get mentally tough. Navigating choppy waters isn't easy. Staying on course in a storm isn't easy. The Greek here literally reads to "gird up the loins of your mind." Men wore layered tunics and cloaks in Jesus' day, but if you had some work to do, you would tie your tunic around your waist to free up your legs. "Girding your loins" would be like us saying, "Roll up your sleeves." You want to be a Jesus follower in tough times? Roll up your sleeves!

My grandson Maddox is a really good ping-pong player, but he is not as good as the Great and Mighty Papa . . . yet. I keep the game roughly even until we both have 18 points, and then I kick it in. I will never let him win. It isn't like that in my family. We were playing a couple of weeks back, and with me serving, he almost beat me, and he would have, had he not missed the end of the table by an eighth of an inch. When I got the final point, he hit the table with his paddle in frustration. I told him, "You can't work for your emotions.

17

You have to put your emotions to work for you. Pull them in. Channel them. Let them make you better. What we don't control will control us." When he learns to do that, the tide in our ping-pong rivalry will begin to change. Peter is saying the exact same thing to his readers. In difficult times Christians must be mentally tough. What we don't control will control us.

What controls our minds controls our perceptions, and what controls our perceptions becomes our reality. The Christian must allow God's Word—not feelings, fear, frustration, cultural pressure, or circumstances—to control our minds. Spiritual toughness means keeping a Christian perspective in front of us at all times and in all seasons! The persecuted members of the early church were cultural pariahs, losing their livelihoods, facing arrest, being ostracized from their social circles, finding their homes looted, or being paraded in front of hungry animals in the Roman Colosseum. For some, the "just made the Jesus team" luster was wearing off, and they wondered just how much more they could endure for this newfound faith. Peter tells them to channel their emotions and remember that any pain suffered for Christ in this world will be greatly rewarded in the world to come. Jesus had once looked at a raging Sea of Galilee when all his disciples were panicking and said, "Silence! Be still!" (Mark 4:39). In the storms of life, we need to allow Jesus to speak his peace into our lives.

Get yourself under control. The Greek word used here means to be sober or to have a sober mind. This means sticking to the charts even when the plan doesn't appear to be working or the price seems much higher than anticipated. I have a fast life hack: never make important decisions during a down cycle. Have you ever noticed that when life is at its worst, humans often make particularly bad decisions? How many people get out of one bad relationship and instinctively jump into a worse one? How many people have hardship come their way and crawl inside a bottle or a medicine cabinet? How many people have financial problems, so they head to the casino? How many people have family trouble, so they find reasons not to go home? Exercising self-control keeps us from making bad decisions in haste and will often keep us from "jumping out of the frying pan and into the fire."

Visualize success. Too many of us spend our lives looking backward. The lostness resulting from the mistakes of yesterday drown out our hopes for charting a better tomorrow. When I ran high hurdles in high school, I learned the secret of visualizing success. Each night before bed, I successfully ran set after set in my mind. When the gun went off in a meet, I simply had to repeat physically what I had accomplished mentally a hundred times before. I learned to run in anticipation of success. The Bible says we reap what we sow, but we don't reap today what we sow today; we reap today what we sowed yesterday, and we will reap tomorrow what we sow today. If you are sowing good stuff but not reaping good stuff, hang on! Look forward to the blessing that is about to come your way. That is what Paul was talking about in Galatians 6:9: "At the proper time we will reap a harvest if we do not give up" (NIV). John Wesley said that we are to "maintain a full expectation of all the grace—the blessings flowing from the full favor of God." When we live God's way, we can live in anticipation of success. Sometimes we just need to slow down long enough for the blessings to catch up with us!

> So you must live as God's obedient children. Don't slip back into your old ways of living to satisfy your own desires. You didn't know any better then. (1 Peter 1:14)

Choose obedience. A defining characteristic of the mature Christian is obedience to God. There is no path to maturity apart from it. Children often don't see the big picture. All they see is what they want right now, and they will often ignore sound instruction to pursue things to their detriment. It seems that children skin their knees when they don't listen to their parents. Likewise, teenagers skin their hearts. But Christians skin their souls. Remember the story of the Prodigal Son? Had he trusted his father and waited on his inheritance, he would have been a wealthy man for the rest of his life. But because he demanded his inheritance in advance and squandered it, he lived his entire life in the service of his obedient brother. If we live our lives God's way, we will receive the inheritance of God's children. If we demand our own way, what we want is all we will ever receive.

Don't go off the rails. When I was fourteen or so, I went on a guy vacation with my dad to Gatlinburg, Tennessee. One day we drove to the top of Ski Mountain and bought tickets to ride the new Alpine Slide. This ride featured awesome track-wheeled bobsleds that shot down concrete runs winding down the mountain. Dad and I took the ski lift and got lined up. All I could think about was beating my dad to the bottom! The instructor told us how to navigate the course, especially emphasizing that we utilize our brakes before we go into the turns, or we could fly off the track. He demonstrated how to use the brakes by pulling back on the stick, but I wasn't interested. I had no intention of using my brakes. How can you defeat your father using the brakes? After ignoring the instructions, we were off. Predictably, I had an early lead. I glanced at my father and marveled at his tentative nature as he nursed his brakes. As I flew into the first turn, my sled shot out from under me, flipped over the side and off the track, and tumbled down the mountain. I slid about a hundred yards, thoroughly skinning my pride, at which point I was forced to climb over the side and off the track in humiliation. From there I walked a quarter of a mile to the bottom where my victorious father sheepishly awaited me. As I was walking down, the instructor at the top no doubt pointed me out to his next group as a cautionary tale. Perfect.

If we are to become the people that God would have us be as we navigate this treacherous journey through life, we must follow the charts, or we will fly over the rails and be blown off course every time.

> But now you must be holy in everything you do, just as God who chose you is holy. 16 For the Scriptures say, "You must be holy because I am holy." (1 Peter 1:15–16)

Live differently (than the world). The Greek word translated "holy" literally means "different." Holy is a word used to describe the temple, a building different from other buildings; the Sabbath, a day different from other days; and a Christian, a human different from other humans. We experience holiness when our lives form congruence with the purpose for which we were created. To navigate holiness, we must know who we are, know who we were created to be, and have some good clues for getting from here to there. What the world will never understand about traditional, Bible-believing Christians is that we honestly believe our best lives are lived according to the clear and consistent teachings of Scripture. Sounding a counter-cultural moral, ethical, or sexual ethic is not an act of hate. It is an act of love.

> And remember that the heavenly Father to whom you pray has no favorites. He will judge or reward you according to what you do. (1 Peter 1:17)

Get real. God does not judge us according to our potential or intention. God judges us according to our actions. When I was a basketball coach, I could play only five kids at once. Parents of the kids who did not get a lot of playing time spent their non-game nights creating conspiracy theories. Some thought that I just played the kids I liked, the better students, or the children of the pillars of the community. In reality, I played the kids I thought could win us basketball games. God has a mission of offering salvation to the whole world through the life, death, and resurrection of His son, Jesus Christ. He is going to play and bless those Christians and churches who will give their all to accomplish this goal. The second God can't use us, God will bench us. In the end, either you get it done, or you don't. It is just the way it is.

Don't get too attached to the world.

> So, you must live in reverent fear of him during your time here as "temporary residents." (1 Peter 1:17b)

When we become Christians, we become citizens of the Kingdom of God. We are no longer citizens of this world. Earth remains our temporary location, but it is not our final destination. We are warned in Scripture not to become too attached to this world or the things it has to offer. It's not that "you can't take it with you." It's that the rewards of this world aren't worth taking. No one emphasized more than Jesus that you can't both live for heaven and be earthbound.

Financial advisors will tell you that a comfortable retirement isn't won when you are sixty. It is really too late to start. It is won by making strategic, short-term sacrifices in your late twenties and early thirties. If you want to reach the goal, you have to play the long game. It isn't easy, but it is worth it.

Christians must also play for the long game. Jesus said it best himself in Matthew 16:24: "If any wish to come after me, let them deny themselves and take up their cross and follow me."

Questions for Discussion and Reflection

1. Do you have difficulty controlling your emotions and exercising self-control? Write a prayer below that you can use to guide you during tough times.

2. Are you living like the world or like Christ? Write down the ways that you need to deny yourself, take up your cross, and follow Jesus.

3. Of the eight navigation tools in this chapter, which would benefit you by focusing on it the most?

Ransomed and Redeemed

Ransom and redemption are fascinating concepts. Let's lay this out. Someone has to first possess something, and someone else has to "by hook or crook" gain functional possession of that thing. Then the second party attempts to extort the first party to buy back what was already theirs at a price. The price required for payment is called ransom. In the old world, ransom normally came in the context of kidnappings. Someone kidnapped an enfranchised person and tried to get the people who loved them to pay for that person's release. We hear more these days about ransomware. Ransomware illegally possesses the contents of your computer and attempts to sell them back to you. The big question is, "How badly do you want back what I have that is yours?" Keep in mind that you never have to pay ransom if you are willing to lose what has been stolen from you. Imagine you have your computer backed up, and nothing on it contains any sensitive information. You might well say to the cyber-kidnapper, "Not paying a cent. Get lost. It is all yours." You pay ransom only for things you love, that you need, or that you don't want others to have. Finally, when the ransom is paid and the stolen person, access, or content is fully returned to its rightful owner, what was taken for ransom has been redeemed.

The gospel story is a redemption story.

As we continue to navigate 1 Peter, we should always remain conscious of its highly pressurized historical context. Christian persecution by the empire was first limited to Rome, but by this point in Peter's life, not only has persecution spread to Peter's audience in northeastern Asia, but it is intensifying. Like many Old Testament prophecies, the message to God's people is, "Things are bad and likely to get worse. Stay faithful, for there are better, even glorious, times ahead. And if they don't come on earth, they will come in heaven." It's with that context that we continue to engage with chapter 1.

So respect him. (1 Peter 1:17b)

This verse can be equally translated "So fear him" or "So stand in awe of him." God is worthy of our awe, our reverence, and our respect. I think there is a clear line between legalism and respectful reverence toward God. Legalism will always look to measurables and observables, like what you wear or how you look, but respect is an attitude of the heart. Some religious traditions don't allow men to wear short sleeves or belts or women to wear jewelry or makeup out of respect for God, and they are free to do as they see fit. I am not about to get on the Amish for being Amish or the Pentecostals for being Pentecostal. If buttons and no zippers on your winter jacket better connect you to Jesus, more power to you. That being said, I am not going to do any of that. I don't think church should be stuffy, but I do believe that a modicum of respect for a place set apart as "holy" should be in the mix somewhere. I would suspect that a person could be legalistic but not reverent and another could be reverent but not legalistic.

One of the things that will surprise you about 1 Peter, especially if you are familiar with the book of James, is its rich theological content. Let's lean in there for a moment and begin by defining theology. Theology is a compound word that literally translates to "the study of God." We often think of theology as abstract, but nothing could be further from the truth. Theology is a lot like navigation. It remains theoretical until we put it to use, and then it is the most practical thing in the world. Theology is the touchpoint at which our faith in God and the unfolding of our human lives intersect. It is where the rudder of the boat meets the water! For me, my standing beliefs about God and my reality concerning those beliefs are always in conversation, and they can break out into an argument. Imagine that I believe that if people are living for God, things will always go well for them. There are entire theological traditions built around this notion. Now imagine that I preach this every week and cherry-pick the Bible verses that support my proposition. In time many people may grow to believe this very fervently, but that doesn't make it true. This is a belief system that won't hold up over the long haul. Bad things happen in a fallen world. Do fewer bad things happen if you are not doing dumb crap? Absolutely, but bad things are still going to happen to good and righteous people through no fault of their own. And did I mention that everyone eventually dies and most of them get sick first? There is that. God will never let you down, but bad theology will let you down eight days a week. In tough times you especially need good theology.

Finally, keep in mind that Peter is giving his persecuted readers the most important stuff. What we are about to explore is a succinct summarization of the gospel message. Here is the "main stuff."

> For you know that God paid a ransom to save you from the empty life you inherited from your ancestors. And the ransom he paid was not mere gold or silver. (1 Peter 1:18)

To be empty is to be devoid of matter, but in a theological sense, it is to be devoid of what matters. Peter may have been arguing concerning the emptiness of rote religion like the Jews practiced or the emptiness of paganism that the Gentiles practiced, or he may have been arguing both. This reminds us that you can miss a bull's eye high or low, left or right. Peter further states that an earthly existence limited to time and space is an empty life. You can barely survive and be empty, or you can be rich and be empty. You can deny yourself and be empty, or you can live for pleasure and be empty. There is nothing fulfilling or eternal about life apart from Christ. It is a stolen life for which God paid a staggering ransom for our redemption.

> It was the precious blood of Christ, the sinless, spotless Lamb of God. God chose him as your ransom long before the world began, but now in these last days he has been revealed for your sake. (1 Peter 1:19–20)

The ransom price to redeem us is the blood of Jesus Christ. He becomes the once-and-for-all perfect sacrificial lamb of Judaism, which was annually sacrificed at Passover to atone for the sins of the people. Furthermore, this was not a knee-jerk adjustment to an unanticipated Fall in the Garden of Eden, but a plan that rested in the heart of God from before the time of creation. How could God have a plan for redemption before the kidnapping? Because God is God! Why is it hard for us to understand? Because we are not God.

> Through Christ you have come to trust in God. And you have placed your faith and hope in God because he raised Christ from the dead and gave him great glory. (1 Peter 1:21)

There are several competing visions for the central message of the gospel. They come from the theological left, right, and center. This is not to mention the right-center and the left-center. For some, the gospel message looks like social transformation; for others, traditional morality and ethics; for others, inner peace; and for others, material success. These things may all be good and well, but the central message of the gospel is that forgiveness of sin and the gift of eternal salvation are made available to us by the resurrection of Jesus. We access this eternal gift by faith, trusting in God's plan for our salvation.

> You were cleansed from your sins when you obeyed the truth, so now you must show sincere love to each other as brothers and sisters. Love each other deeply with all your heart. (1 Peter 1:22)

The text says that we are cleansed of sin through faith on the front side and obedience to God on the back side. There was an old hymn that asked the musical question, "Are you washed in the blood of the Lamb?" Ritual washing was a major part of Judaism because it served as a living metaphor for sin being washed away. Washing in water can render a body clean for a short time. Washing in the blood of Christ can clean a soul for all time.

I am grateful that I was raised in a Christian tradition that emphasized personal salvation. Yet I remember as a child thinking that I had peaked as a Christian because I was already saved and knew the Bible stories. There seemed nothing to do now but wait to die and go to heaven. "What is next?" is a fair question to ask once someone has received Christ. The answer is that through salvation we are adopted into the family of the Church of Jesus Christ, and we are to love one another—not just say we love each other but become completely invested in that love. Saying we love God and failing to love people is not a Christian option. If we don't love one another, we don't love God enough.

> For you have been born again, but not to a life that will quickly end. Your new life will last forever because it comes from the eternal, living word of God. (1 Peter 1:23)

The term "born again" is not new to the New Testament. Jesus told Nicodemus in John 3 that he must be born again. The idea implied in the Greek is that through spiritual rebirth we take on a new nature that reflects our new status. Paul often talked about taking off our worldly nature and putting

29

on the nature of Christ. We are not saved because we love people; we love people because we are saved. When we love people like our Heavenly Father loves people, we are a "chip off the old block"!

> As the Scriptures say, "People are like grass; their beauty is like a flower in the field. The grass withers and the flower fades. But the word of the Lord remains forever." (1 Peter 1:24–25)

This is a succinct quote of Isaiah 40:6–8, in which Isaiah is also talking about the redemption of Israel and being captive to sin. Juxtaposed here is the "don't blink or you will miss it" nature of human life and the eternal nature of the word of God.

The new iPhone apparently has some very powerful filters on its camera, which can do all kinds of things, including making you look younger. In my opinion, the filters distort, and the photos sometimes look like an episode of "plastic surgery gone wrong." This raises the question, would I rather look old or ridiculous? Right now I am opting for old, but I will let you know in a few years.

Peter argues that temporal or youthful beauty may be impressive in its season, but it eventually withers and fades . . . with or without filters. We can fight it, but in the end, human existence comes with a shelf life, and we are going to either lose the battle or end up looking like a character from Batman. God's plan of salvation is not given to style, trend, or fashion and will be just as beautiful in a billion years as it is right now.

And that word is the Good News that was preached
to you. (1 Peter 1:25b)

As Peter drills down into the gospel to address a temporary persecution of his church, four eternal points emerge:

Four Eternal Points

1. Salvation was God's plan.
2. Salvation comes through faith in Christ.
3. Love of others is the fruit of salvation.
4. True reality is eternally with God.

I have always liked baseball, and I have always liked baseball cards. I don't own thousands of cards, but the cards I do have are of high quality. My limited card collection includes personal favorites of players who played when I was a kid. Players such as Tom Seaver, Jerry Koosman, Bob Gibson, Johnny Bench, Roberto Clemente, Willie Mays, and Hank Aaron filled my childhood collection. When I felt called to seminary in 1989, Melissa and I liquidated our meager assets to make the move to Georgia. I remember taking my cards to a collectables show and selling them for seminary money. Terrible.

Upon graduation three years later, I started using wedding money to buy my cards back—not the exact same cards, of course, but cards of the same player and year that I had previously possessed. Not only that, but I eventually upgraded and expanded to include players who came up in the thirties, forties, and fifties. My baseball card collection today is a story of redemption. I had it, I lost it, I got it back, and I have no intention of letting it go. We too are redemption stories. God had us, God lost us, Jesus paid the ransom for us, and God has us back. And you want to know the best news of all? God has no intention of ever letting us go!

 ## Questions for Discussion and Reflection

1. Do you know what it means to balance reverence and fear toward God?

2. How have you changed since becoming a Christian? Are you a "chip off the old block" of God?

Shooting below the Waterline

The vast majority of Jews in the time of Peter did not live in what the Romans called Palestine and we call Israel. Pockets of Jews resided all over the Roman Empire. The preponderance of first-century synagogues, signifying the presence of at least ten Jewish families, discovered by archeologists all around the Mediterranean, testify to this fact. While Jewish Christians had been enduring sporadic harassment for three decades from the Jewish temple and Romans, persecution was a new and painful experience for Gentile Christians. As oppression and fear threatened to quell the expanding Christian movement, Peter wrote this general letter of encouragement to be circulated among the churches of Asia Minor. Peter's love for the people to whom he writes is undeniable, and if his heart breaks for the pain they are enduring, it breaks even more for the additional pain they are about to endure.

Peter understands that the greatest threat to the Christian movement was not from the outside. It was from within. Peter is calling his audience to "step up their game" in the face of increasing persecution. Sin inside the church is a cannonball aimed well below the waterline. Sin in the church hinders our mission, produces internal division, and tarnishes our witness to the world. Sin within the church must be eradicated with extreme prejudice because it doesn't just impact an individual: it impacts the ministry of the whole church! Make no mistake, "loose lips" do indeed sink ships.

Sports roughly divide into individual and team sports. Between high school and college, I lettered four sports divided equally between the two. I loved running high hurdles and playing tennis because it was all on you. You either got it done or didn't. But I also loved football and baseball because you were contributing to something bigger than yourself. Christianity is fascinating because our relationship with God through Christ is personal, but the context in which we live out that faith, the church, is very much relational. Because of that reality, no member of the church can claim that their bad behavior affects only themselves. Bad actors hurt everyone. Bad players impact everyone on the team.

What we are about to explore is God's word to all who comprise the Church of Jesus Christ. Sometimes God loves on us, and sometimes God shoves on us. This is the shoving part.

> So get rid of all evil behavior. Be done with all deceit, hypocrisy, jealousy, and all unkind speech.
> (1 Peter 2:1)

The Greek word translated "rid yourselves" means to "strip off." There are lots of places in the Bible where the metaphor of "putting on" or "stripping off" is used. These accounts carry the clear connotation that we are not beasts driven by undeniable natural instincts on one hand or mindless drones of predestination on the other. We have a choice concerning our actions.

Have you ever done a dirty job? The worst for me is the annual cleaning of our outdoor waterfall feature at my home.

Each spring I drain the water and wade into a lower basin about the size of a hot tub and hand-scoop about five inches of muck and mire from the bottom. It takes about an hour. When I am done, I am a muddy, stinking mess, and my clothes are filthy! In the same way we strip off soiled clothes, Christians are to strip off evil behavior. What constitutes evil behavior? Peter specifically denotes deceit, hypocrisy, jealousy, and unkind speech. All churches are filled with those four things, yet most Christians don't consider any of these to be the "worst" of sins. We save that moniker for sins that we are far less predisposed to commit or sins committed by others. This is a problem.

"Evil" refers to human behavior devoid of Christ. Keep in mind that the ultimate biblical punishment is not God harshly disciplining his people with plague or exile, but it is God removing his presence. When God's presence is removed, evil is what remains. And evil, like weeds in a garden or cancer in a body, will take over if not treated with urgency. Peter opens by listing four evils that threaten the church. We must assume the four things presented are the "primary" threats Peter sees. They are as common today as they were in the first century.

When I was a boy, I often heard sin divided into "sins of omission" and "sins of commission." It still makes lots of sense to me. Sins of omission are things we should do but don't, like ignoring biblical discipleship mandates or God promptings. Sins of commission are things we do that we should not, like engaging in practices the Bible clearly and consistently forbids. The four sins Peter is about to share with us are common sins of commission that pose an uncommon threat to the church.

Four Sins of Commission

1. Deceit. The Greek word that is translated "deceit" has more to do with untoward motives than untoward actions. The first sin of the New Testament church was a sin of deceit when a man named Ananias and his wife Sapphira lied concerning the proceeds of some property they had sold. Acts 5 tells us that they told the disciples they had given all the proceeds from the sale, but in reality they had kept most back for themselves. Peter said, "Why in the world would you attempt to deceive us? You allowed Satan into your heart! You are free to give whatever you wish or don't wish, but you are not free to lie to the Holy Spirit." Ananias dropped dead, and later, when his wife was confronted with the deception, she dropped dead as well. Moral of the story? Deception is not okay in the church.

2. Hypocrisy. This word comes from the Greek word for an actor and literally means "to wear a mask." It was really a neutral word for a disguise until Jesus got ahold of it. Publicly calling religious leaders hypocrites was a favorite pastime of Jesus, and the term was always used in the extreme negative. For Jesus, a hypocrite denoted someone who put out some effort to appear to be something they are not. It is probably best stated in the expression "a wolf in sheep's clothing." This is deceit taken to the next level as it shifts from attitude to action. I define hypocrisy as the "distance between who we are and who we claim to be."

Jealousy. Jealousy wants what is not ours to have and resents those we perceive to have those things. The word used for this third sin, which can also be rendered "envy," reared its ugly head in Jesus' inner circle. Even as Jesus celebrated his last Passover with his disciples in an upper room in Jerusalem, they broke into an argument about "who is the greatest." James and John even had Mommy pull some strings to try to secure a place for her sons above the others. Jealousy cannot only thrust us into a cycle of ungodly ambition but can misinform our perceptions. Jealous people don't see or think clearly. The results are often tragic.

An old story tells about a murder of crows found dead in a field on the hottest day anyone had ever seen in Kansas. The crows had been flying over a popcorn field when the temperature became so sizzling that the kernels began popping right off the husks! The crows looked down, thought it was snowing, and all froze to death. When people are in the grip of jealousy, faulty perception becomes reality, and when people begin to act upon false assumptions, the hull of the gospel ship starts taking on water fast.

Backstabbing. The Greek word means *evil speaking*. Backstabbing is the attempted assassination of the character of another Christian, in which you appear to be a friend to a person's face but speak evil words behind his or her back. "Stabbed in the back" means to be betrayed from the blindside, and I would guess that every one of us carries a few scars. Backstabbing within the church is a despicable act of cowardice, a triumph of Satan, and an absolute failure of Christian community.

We have had occasions in the past in which some vicious gossip about someone or untrue report about something got completely out of hand. When things like that finally get to me, I tell people to "go down into the hole" and get at the root of it. All cannonballs are shot from a single cannon. All of them. When we do that, we normally discover that the fuse was lit not by a person intending evil but by simply someone with hurt feelings, a jealous heart, or wrong information who couldn't keep his or her mouth shut. Others passed the information along assuming it to be true.

When we were a United Methodist Church, I was under the appointment of a bishop who could technically move me at any time. About fifteen years back, someone contacted me congratulating me on being named the pastor of another church. The problem was that it was news to me. This was before the days when ball players learn they have been traded on Twitter. I explained that such rumors are a distraction to me and hurt the mission of Christ Church, and for them to spread untrue gossip was not acceptable. With that I went down into the hole. A few phone calls later, I found the source. Someone trying to do harm? No. But someone who did harm when someone they were talking to interpreted their idle speculation to be a fact, and things got out of control from there. I needed them to know that this was not okay.

Peter is letting his churches know that whether intentional or unintentional, sinful actions inside the church are not to be tolerated. So what do Christians do with information that comes our way?

 ## Handling Information

Is the information true?

Is the information yours to share?

Why do you feel the need to share?

Is your need to share worth the risk of sinning?

Will any good come from sharing?

Will God be honored by sharing?

Sin inside the church is a cannonball shot below the waterline of the gospel ship. You first have to bail the water, assess the damage, and then patch it up. Then you have to go down into the hole to identify the saboteur so that it doesn't happen again. We have all been hit by cannonballs that we didn't see coming, sometimes fired by people we would never expect to betray or attempt to do us harm. I know I have. How does the church protect herself against the deceit, hypocrisy, jealousy, and backstabbing that are inevitable in a fallen world? What do we do to those who intentionally or unintentionally fire the cannon? How do Christian people who have been wounded heal, and how does the church repair the damage to the hull and recover its mission? I don't know where it ends, but it begins by taking it to Jesus. We have all inflicted hurt. We are all damaged. Jesus came so we wouldn't have to stay that way.

Questions for Discussion and Reflection

1. Is there an action or attitude that you need to rid yourself of?

2. Gossip is a dangerous and often accepted sin within a church. What can you do to help be a voice of truth and restraint against gossip?

Spoiled and Spilled Milk

If I had to denote a single word to describe the shift in my worldview over the past decade, it would be "outnumbered." Though the word "persecution" is way too strong to describe what I have experienced as a traditional Christian, knowing that my core beliefs around Scripture and convictions around things such as human sexuality and abortion make me "the problem" in the eyes of many is new to me. Knowing that anything I say on anything that contradicts the prevailing current social narrative can either get me censored or ignite a social media firestorm is new to me. Knowing that the constant volatility of our culture and that the no-win leadership scenario is the new normal is new to me. But even as bad as it all feels sometimes, I have endured nothing compared to what many Christians in the New Testament began to experience the moment they professed their faith in Christ. Many of these folks lost their reputations, livelihoods, families, and homes. Some lost their lives. These suffering believers are the people to whom Peter writes.

So how do people of faith navigate waters far more troubled than they ever imagined possible? What do Christians do when persecution is suddenly upon them? When such times come, how do we respond to our detractors, accusers, slanderers, and persecutors? For Peter, you begin by shoring things up within the church and watching your spiritual diet. These are clear warnings that a healthy Christian community in a fallen world must be maintained with vigilance.

A few weeks before Thanksgiving, a snake entered the cabin we call our home. Melissa saw it first and thought it was a rope. It was not a rope. I am not afraid of snakes, but I really don't want to touch one either. By the time I found some spaghetti tongs to get him, he disappeared. It took up residence in the basement furnace room and seemed to have access to both the walls and ceiling. Melissa named him Randall. We would see him every so often but couldn't seem to catch him. He wasn't poisonous and didn't seem to be doing any harm, but you can't have a snake slithering wild in your house. After trying about ten things that they said to do on the internet and calling an exterminator, I finally caught him, but that does not mean another snake won't one day find its way in. We live in a cabin in the middle of woods that is the home to many snakes. Snakes will be more of a tension to be managed than a problem to be solved. Our task is to make it as hard as possible for Randall's kin to get in and to be as vigilant as possible to get them out should they enter. The relationship between the church and sin works about the same way.

Satan is an adversary of the people of God. Satan works desperately, trying to keep us from advancing in our mission of connecting people to Jesus Christ. Satan wants the church distracted, divided, ineffective, and consumed with non-missional things. One of those things is interior conflict.

Two front wars are hard to win, and many churches and denominations unsuccessfully attempt to fight both the devil and one another. Imagine that a new person visits a conflicted church and is touched by God in a profound way. How long do you think it will take before people attempt to drag that new believer into their conflict and ask that person to take sides? Possibly minutes. Instead of being welcomed into a loving Christian community, people are informed as to the content of their new causes and given updates on who their new enemies ought to be. I wonder how many people have come to Jesus and four minutes later were drawn into a localized scrap about the style of the music in church. We all know how the story ends. The new believer will be gone in a month, and the learning curve from those folks in the church will be zero. The same thing will happen the next time. Conflict in a church isn't much of a threat to evangelism, but it will destroy discipleship. People can't root in toxic soil.

No ship can be effective if the crew is fighting with the captain or with one another. One of the things I have learned in over three decades of church work is that conflict within churches and between Christians is inevitable. I have also learned that whether conflict destroys a church or strengthens a church depends on how conflict is handled. Jesus offered a clear process to work through conflict in Matthew 18.

> If another believer sins against you, go privately and
> point out the offense. (Matthew 18:15a)

This counterintuitive teaching addresses how those in the church should treat others in the church with whom they have become cross-threaded. Imagine someone in the church has deeply offended you. What do you do? Sometimes doing nothing is the right thing. I actively refuse to get offended by people if I can possibly avoid it, but Melissa constantly reminds me that I have the hide of an elephant and most people don't. So, if someone without malintent offends and you are thick-skinned enough to overlook it, you probably should. But if the hurt is so deep that you need to talk about it for you to heal, you no longer have the choice of inaction. Your choice now is obedience to God or disobedience to God. Tragically, many people deal with hurt by talking to everyone but the person who hurt them. This is sin. It is a cannonball below the waterline of the church. Such behavior cannot be tolerated, or the mission of the church will be compromised. Jesus taught us when we are offended and can't shake it off that we are to go directly to the person who offended us and have a calm and honest conversation around the point of offense. This is the hardest possible option and the only Christian option. So, if you can't keep it to yourself or feel you shouldn't keep it to yourself, you must take it to the person who offended you and keep in mind that texting or email is the worst possible way to do it.

> If the other person listens and confesses it, you have
> won that person back. (Matthew 18:15b)

I have found that disagreement in a church is more often a matter of misunderstanding, insensitivity, or a failure to communicate than a matter of maliciousness. However, the effects are all about the same. Whether you run over a dog on purpose or accidentally, it is all about the same to the dog. If the cause is insensitivity or miscommunication and the desired outcome is reconciliation and not retribution, the relationship can be healed and even strengthened.

But if you are unsuccessful, take one or two others with you and go back again, so that everything you say may be confirmed by two or three witnesses. (Matthew 18:16)

Now some time has elapsed, and there are witnesses in place to move the situation toward agreement. Have you ever looked back on a heated conflict and realized if you had just held your tongue or not gotten defensive, things would have gone differently? Often the content of a disagreement is very solvable, but the attitudes and posturing of the people in the discussion never allow things to be resolved. I am a firm believer in letting "cooler heads prevail." Usually, when there are referees around, the players behave better!

 If the person still refuses to listen, take your case to the church. (Matthew 18:17a)

Remember that this is conflict resolution for Christian people. The buck stops with the spiritual authority of those whom God has entrusted to leadership within the church. If they humbly accept the decision, fellowship is maintained, but . . .

 Then if he or she won't accept the church's decision, treat that person as a pagan or a corrupt tax collector. (Matthew 18:17b)

Many churches have died because Christians refuse to handle things as Jesus taught us. Doing evangelism, discipleship, and ministry in a fallen world is hard work, but if the leaders do not enforce church discipline, it is impossible work. The Greek literally reads, if people refuse the authority of the church, treat them like a "pagan or corrupt tax collector." They would be people who would have to repent and show a change of behavior to be received into the church. On the other hand, Jesus treated these folks really well! The idea here is to shift your thinking toward those who will not accept the authority of the church community from member to prospect.

I believe that the most prevalent threat to any church comes from the inside, not the outside. The ocean floor is filled with churches who let people shoot cannonballs below the waterline and pastors who would rather go down with the ship than confront their saboteurs. When being "nice" becomes a higher core value than being "obedient," a church is taking on water already.

So, what becomes of people who have gotten caught up in sins such as deceit, hypocrisy, jealousy, and backstabbing that destroy churches? Jesus gave us a clear path to repentance, forgiveness, and restoration.

A Path to Relational Restoration

If your sins are against God, confess them to God.

If your sins are against someone else and they are aware of your sin against them, confess to God and ask for forgiveness from that individual.

If your sin is against an individual and they are not aware of it, confess your sin to God and ask forgiveness from those to whom you have spoken evil about another person.

Now "go and sin no more"!

I discovered long ago that if Christian leaders don't keep the wolves at bay, feeding the sheep soon becomes a theoretical exercise. The bottom line is that dead sheep don't eat much. Now that Peter has taught us how to deal with wolves, he can turn his attention toward instructing us in how to feed the sheep.

> Like newborn babies, you must crave pure spiritual milk so that you will grow into a full experience of salvation. Cry out for this nourishment, now that you have had a taste of the Lord's kindness. (1 Peter 2:2–3)

Rather than the churches craving sinful things, Peter encourages his churches to crave the pure gospel of Jesus Christ! He realizes that our outputs are directly related to our inputs. What goes in is what comes out. Babies are interesting. They have a skill set consisting of only two things. They eat stuff, something happens to the stuff, and modified stuff comes out. If there is too much sin coming out of you, Peter would suggest a new diet called "pure spiritual milk." We can uncover the items on the new diet by reversing the four sins we explored earlier. Instead of eating junk food such as deceit, hypocrisy, jealousy, and backstabbing, we should maintain a healthy diet of truth, authenticity, and honor and support of one another. If you want to grow babies into strong kids, you have to feed them well. If you want to grow spiritual babies into strong Christians, you have to feed them well.

The final point is that once you taste good "milk," you will never drink a drop of spoiled milk again. This reminds us of the importance of studying Scripture! Scripture is the kind of food that enables a brand-new believer to grow into a man or woman of God.

To what things are you subjecting yourself the other six days and twenty-two hours a week when you are not in church? If garbage is going in, I assure you that garbage is coming out. If good stuff is going in, I assure you that good stuff is coming out. If you want to change your outputs, change your inputs. Are you always radiating at high speeds about the world around you? Is it turning you into an angry person? You need to read more Bible, find some new voices to speak into your heart, and watch less news. Are you struggling with lust, infidelity, sexual temptation, or pornography? You need to ask God to deliver you, deny yourself access to that stuff, and turn your heart to godly, wholesome, and uplifting things. Are you falling victim too often to sins such as deceit, hypocrisy, jealousy, and backstabbing? You need to learn to recognize those impulses, keep your mouth shut and your fingers still, and nip that stuff in the bud. You get the idea. We often ask for God to deliver us as if we have no role to play in the matter. The fact is that we each choose whether we are drinking pure milk or spoiled milk.

Navigating Christianity in Challenging Times

Stand in eternal hope.

Realize that trials purify us.

Live holy "set apart" lives.

Reject emotions and words that tear down Christian community.

Embrace emotions and words that build up community.

Desire the Word of God.

May I close the chapter with a quote from Jesus of Nazareth? He said this in a final meal with his apostles where Satan wanted nothing more than to spoil and spill the milk.

"So now I am giving you a new commandment: Love each other. Just as I have loved you, you should love each other. Your love for one another will prove to the world that you are my disciples."
(John 13:34–35)

Questions for Discussion and Reflection

1. Is there someone who has sinned against you that you have not gone to privately to discuss? Have you considered how this has affected you?

2. Check your inputs. Are you subjecting yourself to things that are not honoring to God? Take an inventory and decided what needs to be removed and what needs to be added.

Stumbling Over Jesus

When we are on pilgrimage to the Holy Land, our head guide, Mike, often refers to Jerusalem as a city of living stones. Mike is referring to the quarried and carefully cut stones used to build the layers, walls, and structures that have defined the Holy City for millennia. For him, these stones live. They offer praise, they weep, and they dance. In the same way that stones are the building blocks of Jerusalem, those who place their trust in Jesus are the living stones comprising a New Jerusalem. Shockingly, the rejected and crucified Jesus Christ is the cornerstone of this kingdom. It is he who holds the Old Testament and the New Testament together. It is for him that the "rocks cry out"!

Psalm 118 is the foundation for 1 Peter 2:11–12. Psalm 118 is a robust song of praise, deliverance, and thanksgiving to God. It opens with, "Give thanks to the Lord for he is good! His faithful love endures forever." The tone of the Psalm is joyful, and it boasts of God's mighty deeds. It extols the power of a God who brings faith from fear, victory from defeat, and life from death. And so great is the Lord that he is utterly bewildering to humans. The ultimate expression of this confounding nature of God is found in Psalm 118:22–23: "The stone that the builders rejected has now become the cornerstone. This is the Lord's doing, and it is wonderful to see." When stones were cut for ancient structures, some ended up not passing inspection. The Psalmist proclaims that by the power of God, a rejected stone has become the exalted cornerstone. The connotation is, "Only God could do something like that, and who could have possibly seen it coming?"

If the verses that we explore seem different from what we have encountered so far, it is because this is a metaphor. Peter paints a mental picture of the fledgling Church of Jesus Christ as a "New Temple," and both Jewish and Gentile Christians are the living stones who comprise her. This is difficult material for us, but it would not have been for Peter's readers. Everything in their frame of reference would have made these metaphors and their implications an easy grasp. That being said, almost nothing in our frame of reference makes this metaphor and its implications an easy grasp.

You are coming to Christ, who is the living cornerstone of God's temple. He was rejected by people, but he was chosen by God for great honor.
(1 Peter 2:4)

People had always come to the temple in Jerusalem to find God, and now they were coming to Christ. This is a metaphor Jesus applied to himself in Matthew 21:42, Mark 12:10, and Luke 20:17. Since "Jesus as Cornerstone" is recorded in all three Synoptic Gospels, it must have been a reference Jesus used regularly. No one could have had any idea what he was talking about thirty years back, but now it seemed much clearer. Jesus of Nazareth, rejected by his own people and crucified by the Romans thirty years prior, had now become the cornerstone of the Christian movement. Most importantly,

God was in it! The Church of Jesus Christ is the "New Temple." God now dwells in the hearts of all believers, not just in a building built by Herod the Great in Jerusalem. The Old and the New Covenant are two walls joined together by the cornerstone of Jesus Christ!

Peter's Four Essential Claims

1. Jesus is central to our faith. If the church is not built on the life, death, and resurrection of Jesus Christ, the church is not the church. Jesus must be our foundation, and our faith must be built upon the Christ that is testified to in the Bible.

2. Jesus is alive. The church is not a dead and inanimate thing, like a quarried limestone building block, but something vibrant, alive, and active in time and space. Jesus is not a dead prophet or teacher. Jesus is alive, and because he lives, so too can we live!

3. The Church is the New Temple. The Jerusalem temple was the heart of Jewish life and community. There were many synagogues but only one temple. This new temple is defined not by a geographical place but by the very presence of Christ.

4. The Church is bigger than we are. A building block becomes significant only when it is a part of something bigger than itself. Until we realize that we are doing something in a community that is bigger than all of us, we will never understand the unique mission of the Church. Now let's see how these claims apply.

> And you are living stones that God is building into his spiritual temple. What's more, you are his holy priests. Through the mediation of Jesus Christ, you offer spiritual sacrifices that please God. As

> the Scriptures say, "I am placing a cornerstone in Jerusalem, chosen for great honor, and anyone who trusts in him will never be disgraced." (1 Peter 2:5)

This is more poetry than prose. Peter evokes eclectic images and ideas everywhere from Exodus 19:5–6 (the holy priesthood) to the contemporary thoughts of communities such as the Essenes' Dead Sea Scrolls concerning a "living Temple." Herod's temple was destroyed in 70 AD because the Jews revolted against Rome in 66 AD. They destroyed it because anything built with human hands is capable of being destroyed, but the Church is a different thing entirely. It is not one building made of inanimate stones standing in a single location in a political hotspot like Jerusalem. The Church of Jesus Christ is composed of living stones and located in the hearts of all believers. Man didn't build it, and man can't tear it down. The New Temple is indestructible.

Temple priests approached God with pomp and circumstance and offered sacrifices on behalf of the people. Priests were buffers who stood between a holy God and a sinful people. Peter argues that because of the ultimate sacrifice of Jesus, individual Christians can now go directly to God anywhere, anytime. This shifts Christianity from a religion once removed to an intimate relationship! The Christians to whom Peter writes are suffering persecution, but Peter reminds them that there is no disappointment for the living stones who comprise the New Temple.

> Yes, you who trust him recognize the honor God has given him. But for those who reject him, "The stone that the builders rejected has now become the cornerstone." And, "He is the stone that makes

people stumble, the rock that makes them fall."
They stumble because they do not obey God's word,
and so they meet the fate that was planned for them.
(1 Peter 2:7–8)

The juxtaposition is between a cornerstone and a stumbling block. A cornerstone holds things together because it is in the right place, and a stumbling block is something that you trip over because it is in the wrong place.

I am going to put this most bluntly. Humanity was created to be in eternal communion with God. The deal was simple: love and obey God, and everything will be great. Reject God, and you are on your own. Because of original sin, the only trail for humanity suddenly led to eternal damnation. Hell is where we are all headed. God was not content to leave us without a remedy, but God offers us another path if we receive Christ into our lives. The saying is sure: "All you have to do to go to hell is nothing."

The work of Jesus Christ will always offer us an alternative trail. You want to go to heaven? You are going to have to do something. Many people consider Jesus Christ as something to trip over rather than build their lives upon. Because of the opportunity that we all have to receive Christ, Christ becomes either our salvation or our missed opportunity for salvation. The only question in our earthly existence that has an eternal impact is, "What did you do with Jesus?" And our response will render Jesus either our cornerstone as we walk in light or our stumbling block as we walk in darkness.

But you are not like that, for you are a chosen people. You are royal priests, a holy nation, God's very own possession. As a result, you can show

others the goodness of God, for he called you out of
the darkness into his wonderful light. (1 Peter 2:9)

Peter writes to those who have chosen the Jesus trail. This verse is largely a direct quote of Exodus 19:6 and continues the New Testament thought that Christians, even Gentile Christians, are the new Israel.

Big Ideas from Verse Nine

You are a chosen people. Peter again re-contextualizes the Old Testament by transferring the unique status of the Old Testament Jews to the New Testament Church of Jesus Christ. We are reminded that we didn't choose God, but God chose us.

We are a kingdom of priests. In the Jerusalem temple, there were places only priests could go. When Jesus was crucified, there was an earthquake, and the curtain that kept people out of the Holy of Holies was split in two. We are told by the historian Josephus that the veil of the temple was a full four inches thick and sewn so well that even horses tied to each end could not split it. Through Christ, God has given each of us unlimited access to the holy things of God! Do you understand what a privilege that is?

We are a holy nation. We are a "New Israel," a people united in Christ and set apart for the special purpose of bringing salvation to the world.

We are called from darkness into light. You stumble in the darkness. You walk with surety in the light.

"Once you had no identity as a people; now you are God's people. Once you received no mercy; now you have received God's mercy." (1 Peter 2:10)

Gentiles had no stake in the promises God made to Israel. Jewish men thanked God every day that they were not born Gentiles. This verse is a "mash-up" quote of Hosea 1:10 and 2:23 and strengthens the argument of God's acceptance of Gentile Christians because of the work of Christ and the mercy of God. Gentiles don't deserve this elevated status of being called God's people. There was no reason to think we could ever achieve it. We are God's people nonetheless.

Dear friends, I warn you as "temporary residents and foreigners" to keep away from worldly desires that wage war against your very souls. Be careful to live properly among your unbelieving neighbors. Then even if they accuse you of doing wrong, they will see your honorable behavior, and they will give honor to God when he judges the world.
(1 Peter 2:11–12)

Despite the excitement of future victory and glory, the battle still rages in time and space, and Peter abruptly brings his readers back down to earth. In an atmosphere of intensifying persecution, slander, and accusations, Peter reminds his church they are being closely and critically watched, and if anything can be taken wrongly, it will be. Their failures will be celebrated, and their successes will be held with skepticism. Optics matter. Even with perfect optics, there will be few immediate wins. The solution to living in a hostile culture is to live blamelessly.

What Does It Mean to Live Blamelessly?

Remember this world is not your home.

Stay away from temptation.

Live in a way that honors God.

Don't feed your worldly desires.

Witness with your actions.

Jesus is the cornerstone that holds the Old and New Testament together. The Old Testament anticipates him, the Gospels introduce him, and the New Testament celebrates him! A consistent theme of the Bible is that walking the path that leads to life is hard, but our lives will bring glory to God. One day we will be vindicated. We started the chapter with a psalm of thanksgiving, so let's conclude with a psalm of vindication from the final stanza of Psalm 23:5–6:

> "You prepare a feast for me in the presence of my enemies. You honor me by anointing my head with oil. My cup overflows with blessings. Surely your goodness and unfailing love will pursue me all the days of my life, and I will live in the house of the Lord forever."

 ## Questions for Discussion and Reflection

1. If someone asked you, "Why did you choose Jesus?" How would you respond?

2. How would you describe living blamelessly?

The Saved, the Suffering, and the Oppressed

For many of us, when we think of a household, we think of a nuclear family, but if you lived in a different age or a different country, you would think very differently. For the house of Bishop, it was Melissa, the two kids, and me, and when the two kids married to establish their own households, it was Melissa and me again. Then Melissa and me and our 200-year-old rescue dog. In the Bible it was different.

In the Old Testament, the story of Jacob is an account of unending complexity within the household of a patriarchal, polygamous desert herdsman with no real place to call home but holding substantial assets. Things are more recognizable to us in the New Testament period. People seem more tethered to a place, they live in structures rather than tents, and political structures are more recognizable. The one thing that never changes is that the more resources you control, the larger your household is going to be. Wealthy households in the Roman Empire included young children, adult children, their families, extended family, servants and slaves, and the families of servants and slaves. Upon first glance servants and slaves looked very much alike. People became slaves in the

Roman Empire for reasons ranging from being part of a conquered people group, to being orphaned or abandoned as a child, to getting yourself too far in debt. People might also sell themselves or their children into slavery in times of economic depression, financial ruin, or famine. Many well-known people of the first century ranging from educators to administrators to entertainers were slaves, but most slaves were worked to death in fields, quarries, building projects, or mines and then discarded and forgotten.

The Romans believed that they were the best civilization in the history of the world. You pushed up against Roman sensibilities to your own peril. Everything and everybody existed for Rome. Agitators, activists, and revolutionaries found themselves hanging on roadsides nailed to Roman crosses, getting their eyes pecked out and skin ripped off by birds to remind the masses of what happens when you mess with Rome. In the Roman mind, the state was the ultimate example of how to live a proper life, and city government, commerce, and individual households were expected to generally follow that hierarchical administrative model. In a sense, an individual household was a micro-empire with the patriarch serving as mini-emperors. It was the Roman way, and it was that or the highway.

Jewish culture and Roman culture were incompatible. As a distinct Christian culture began to emerge in the mid-first century, it wasn't going to be compatible either. The Romans were pretty easy to get along with if you obeyed their laws, respected their gods, generally bought into their system, publicly offered your allegiance to the state, and didn't make waves. But Jews and Christians would not worship the emperor. They offered their ultimate allegiance to God. What the Romans saw as civics, the Christians saw as apostasy. It was problematic.

As a result of both early temple and later Roman persecution, Christians began to scatter all over the empire and took their distinct faith with them. To understand the mentality of 1 Peter, we must understand that the endgame is the spread of the gospel, not the quality of life of the individual. In many cases, "Suck it up for the team" is the motto of team Jesus. Since Peter is writing to both displaced Jewish and recently converted Gentile Christians who were facing ever intensifying persecution from the emperor, he offers very practical instruction in this section. Peter was anything but a social reformer. He felt that bumping up against established norms would just slow down the spread of the gospel. Peter is not offering value judgments on the institutions he is about to address. He is simply advocating keeping the Christian movement alive by limiting things that could lead to increased persecution. Peter is offering advice concerning how to navigate the public living of the Christian faith in a hostile culture. *"Here is how to be a Christian within the constructs of the institutions and social structures in which you live."* This advice is practical and pragmatic. This is not social justice. It is evangelism. *"This is how you need to act to reach other people for Christ . . ."*

> For the Lord's sake, submit to all human authority— whether the king as head of state, or the officials he has appointed. For the king has sent them to punish those who do wrong and to honor those who do right. (1 Peter 2:13–14)

It might be helpful to think of the emperor as the federal government and regional kings or governors as state and local government. Rome set the macro law, but each region enforced it a bit differently. That is why persecution was so intense in some Roman provinces but not in others. The laws were the same across the Mediterranean, but enforcement of those laws was mostly inconsistent. The theoretical aim of the Roman government was to administer justice and serve the common good. Peter seems more than willing to give the prevailing government the benefit of all doubt. His advice is not to resist, retaliate, rebel, or revolt. It is to submit for the greater good of the Christian movement.

> It is God's will that your honorable lives should silence those ignorant people who make foolish accusations against you. For you are free, yet you are God's slaves, so don't use your freedom as an excuse to do evil. Respect everyone, and love the family of believers. Fear God, and respect the king.
> (1 Peter 2:15–17)

There were three groups of people in the Roman Empire: citizens, slaves, and most everyone else. The "most everyone else folks" who converted to Christianity were instructed to live in such a way as it brought honor to God. This would defuse the accusations made against Christians that were baseless lies: "foolish accusations." The use of the word "ignorant" concerning those making the accusations has as much to do with not knowing a thing as being derogative. Christianity was a much maligned and little understood religion. In fact, it was still trying to figure itself out. Rather than seek to understand, ignorant people persecuted. Not much has changed on that front.

The next verses involve how to "silence" ignorant persecution. Keep in mind, Peter is writing only to Christians.

Silencing "Ignorant" Persecution

Keep the endgame in mind (don't misuse freedom).

Live blamelessly (don't do evil).

Be respectful of everyone.

Love your Christian brothers and sisters.

Fear God.

Respect authority.

Though Peter writes to free Christians, he reminds them that to receive Christ is to become a slave to God. Our lives are not our own. You will see from the verses that follow, Peter is not advocating social activism. He is exploring how to be faithful to God within the current social structure. Almost on cue Peter says, *"And speaking of which, here are some really hard things Christians need to do."*

> You who are slaves must submit to your masters with all respect. Do what they tell you—not only if they are kind and reasonable, but even if they are cruel. For God is pleased when, conscious of his will, you patiently endure unjust treatment. Of course, you get no credit for being patient if you are beaten for doing wrong. But if you suffer for doing good and endure it patiently, God is pleased with you. (1 Peter 2:18–20)

Though estimates are all over the place, there were approximately seventy million people in the Roman Empire as of this writing, including about ten million slaves. Slaves could be classified as urban household, rural/agricultural workers, and isolated miners. Slaves could be of any race or people group. This section addresses what I would call "white collar" slaves who were a part of a household. Most of these slaves lived comfortably, ate well, dressed well, and were not treated brutally. Some had education, significant areas of responsibility, and marketable skill sets, and some were even able to earn private money. Of all the categories of slaves, urban household slaves were the most likely to buy their own freedom . . . and many did. Others were freed after years of faithful service. While some of these folks were treated better than the law required, other slaves were not. Some Christian slaves served mentally unstable Roman masters and were abused and treated cruelly by any measure. Some were horribly mistreated during their working lives and freed late in life so that the master would not have to care for them once they became unproductive. They would have been reduced to beggars and, in the absence of a social network, may have died homeless. Well or maltreated, slaves were the legal property of the owner, and the children of slaves were legal commodities.

Christianity was problematic to Roman culture because it taught that Jew or Gentile, rich or poor, slave or free, we all stand equal before God. It was a radically egalitarian notion. The conundrum is obvious. Just how should people who are equal in the eyes of God but unequal in the eyes of the law relate to one another in the church? The answers for Peter were found in an "in here / out there" dichotomy. Here we get a pretty strong statement from Peter: all Christians stand equal in the eyes of God. Period.

Peter instructs Christian slaves to submit to their masters even if they are treated cruelly and unjustly. It was a tough ask, but there was little alternative. The Stoic philosophers of the time basically said to slaves, "This is a bad deal for you, but you need to make the best of it." Peter isn't far from this. He was sympathetic to the plight of slaves, but Roman law was not. Peter believed that the deportment of Christian slaves in obviously unjust situations was a powerful witness. We often think that our best witness is made when our lives are moving "up and to the right." I disagree. I would suggest that our most powerful witness occurs when all hell is breaking loose. When things are so bad that we can't hide it anymore and yet we keep the faith, remain obedient to Jesus, and choose to behave honorably. Peter added that if slaves suffered unjustly, God would bless them for it. The enslaved reader had to be thinking, "You have to be kidding." Peter's response is essentially, "Let me tell you why I am not . . ."

> For God called you to do good, even if it means suffering, just as Christ suffered for you. He is your example, and you must follow in his steps.
> (1 Peter 2:21)

Christians are called to reflect the values of God, even and especially when it is really hard to do. The Greek word for "good" means "thoroughly good." Completely good. The absence of all impurity. Good in all things. The ultimate example of goodness in the face of unjust suffering was Jesus himself. Peter now quotes Isaiah 53 to connect Jesus to the plight of suffering slaves.

The Example of Christ in the Face of Injustice

Jesus didn't suffer because of sin. "He never sinned, nor ever deceived anyone." (1 Peter 2:22)

Jesus did not retaliate. "He did not retaliate when he was insulted . . . "(1 Peter 2:23a)

Jesus did not threaten. ". . . nor threaten revenge when he suffered." (1 Peter 2:23b)

Jesus left justice to God. "He left his case in the hands of God, who always judges fairly." (1 Peter 2:23c)

Slaves are powerless, but God brings justice on behalf of the powerless.

Next Peter shifts from the practical to the theological and from the present to the past by continuing to link Isaiah's suffering servant from chapter 53 with the suffering of Jesus and Jesus with the suffering of Christians in bondage.

> He personally carried our sin in his body on the cross so that we can be dead to sin and live for what is right. By his wounds you are healed. Once you were like sheep who wandered away. But now you have turned to your Shepherd the Guardian of your souls. (1 Peter 2:24–25)

Through the work of the cross, Jesus took our sin, our shame, our disease, and their control over us upon himself, and all of it died with him. Are these sins and evils still with us? Absolutely! They tempt us, but they don't control us. Peter reminds us that though a believer may be trapped without recourse or remedy in a horrific institution such as slavery, spiritual freedom is available in Christ. The Christian slave patiently suffers injustice, not because he is in bondage and has no choice, but because he is free to follow the example of Christ! Obedience to Christ is the ultimate exercise of freedom.

A powerful event is recorded in Luke 4:18. Jesus is at the height of his personal popularity in Galilee and in his "home" synagogue of Nazareth as he reads these words from Isaiah 61:1: "The Spirit of the Sovereign Lord is upon me, for the Lord has anointed me to bring good news to the poor. He has sent me to comfort the brokenhearted and to proclaim that captives will be released, and prisoners will be freed." That freedom for the captives, prophesied by Isaiah and claimed by Jesus, is exactly what Peter has just described.

Questions for Discussion and Reflection

1. How do you react to Peter's lack of willingness to "resist, retaliate, rebel, or revolt" against the Roman government that persecuted Christians?

2. Jesus was the ultimate example of goodness in the face of unjust suffering. Have you or someone you know been a powerful witness for Christ when all hell was breaking loose? What was the situation?

 # Learning to Behave

Peter is offering the members of the churches of Asia Minor advice for their personal behavior during times of persecution. We used to call public behavior "deportment" when I was in elementary school. Were I to sum 1 Peter up, I would offer, "Being a Christian is going to cause you plenty of trouble all by itself; don't add to it." Peter has advised Christians that this world is not their home. As they live as "temporary aliens," they are to respect governmental authority. Free people are to treat everyone as brothers and sisters, and slaves are to accept the authority of their masters. Clearly, Peter's intent is to make sure that the spreading of the gospel throughout the Roman world is not slowed down. He is an evangelist, not a reformer, but his sympathies clearly lie with the oppressed. Now he follows the same general pattern to address wives, husbands, and Christians in general.

Before we get started, we do well to get our heads around how marriage worked in the Roman Empire. As I have previously pointed out, the governmental system of Rome was seen as ideal, and every institution, including the family, was expected to follow it. In his own home, the husband or the patriarch was the emperor. The later axiom "A man is the king of his castle" is rooted in this understanding. In a legal sense, young girls were the property of their fathers, and they were transferred to be the property of their husbands upon marriage. As far as women were concerned, marriage really wasn't that much different than slavery from a legal standpoint. Wives were expected to obey their husbands after marriage as they had obeyed their fathers before. They were expected to keep their opinions to themselves and not really have original thoughts on anything. That a wife would convert to Christianity without her husband doing so would be scandalous. The surrounding drama would be the sort of household disruption that a Roman most frowned upon.

This explains why a major critique of Christianity in the Roman Empire was that the movement was "anti-family." Were I to list three virtues for a wife that the empire held dear, they would be respectful, virtuous, and silent. Clearly, there was a fidelity and devotion expected from married women that did not apply to their husbands. It was once said of southern Illinois in the early 1800s that it was heaven for "men and horses" and hell for "women and oxen." Marriage worked the same way back then. Women lived in a very small box under constant surveillance, and men did as they pleased. Though there were some great marriages featuring deep love, partnership, monogamy, devotion, and respect, these featured a far more generous spirit than the law required. Finally, like some slaves, some wives were horribly mistreated and left without recourse or remedy.

> In the same way, you wives must accept the authority of your husbands. Then, even if some refuse to obey the Good News, your godly lives will speak to them without any words. They will be won over by observing your pure and reverent lives.
> (1 Peter 3:1–2)

Many historians think there were more women converts than men converts in the early church. Simply put, men had more to lose by being a member of an unpopular religion. I would guess that for male Gentile converts, the prospect of being circumcised would be a significant filter. Eventually, circumcision was not required, but that came after some time and debate as Christianity slowly emerged from a sect of Judaism to a faith in and of itself. Wives of unbelieving husbands were instructed not to leave their husbands and not to push on the boundaries of Roman marriage too hard. This is a rare biblical instruction of what I call a "silent witness." Peter is imploring Christian wives to honor God by the way they live. This will ensure that unbelieving husbands might be drawn to Christ on one hand, and no criticism could come to them or the church on the other.

 ## Questions for Discussion and Reflection

1. How would you define Christian marriage to a non-believer?

2. Do you treat your spouse the way Peter describes in this chapter?

Christian Wives

Godly.

Submissive.

Pure.

Reverent.

> Don't be concerned about the outward beauty of
> fancy hairstyles, expensive jewelry, or beautiful
> clothes. You should clothe yourselves instead with
> the beauty that comes from within, the unfading
> beauty of a gentle and quiet spirit, which is so
> precious to God. (1 Peter 3:3–4)

This is a juxtaposition between the gaudy and the godly.
Much like today, most people in the empire were not rich, but
the "rich and famous" set the trends of the day, and the Romans were a trendy lot. They felt a part of their role in the
world was to bring civilization and culture to their "lessers,"
which was basically everyone. Fashion was a part of that role.
The city of Rome was Paris, London, and New York all rolled
into one, and fashion trickled down from the capital city to
the residents of the empire. This held especially true in cities
that fashioned themselves as "little Romes." Jewelry has been a
part of the human equation far longer than you might imagine.

Archeologists have found jewelry in burial chambers in almost every ancient culture. This tells us much about the people and the civilization of Rome. Wealthy Roman women braided their hair in elaborate ways and wore lots of "bling" intended to catch the attention of others and offer a clear insight into their status. We know that armbands, necklaces, bracelets, and rings were popular and that women wore lots of them all at once. We also know that Roman moralists raged against over-adornment as destructive vanity. That everyone else copied the "rich and famous" is human nature.

In contrast, Christian wives were encouraged to focus upon inner, spiritual, and relational beauty. This kind of beauty begins on the inside and works its way out. The practice of head coverings and extremely modest clothing for married women is a part of this line of thinking. Your beauty is for your husband. Don't dress in such a way as to call attention to anything other than your commitment to your marriage, the integrity of your character, and to Christ.

> This is how the holy women of old made themselves beautiful. They put their trust in God and accepted the authority of their husbands. For instance, Sarah obeyed her husband, Abraham, and called him her master. You are her daughters when you do what is right without fear of what your husbands might do.
> (1 Peter 3:5–6)

Though the Old Testament is patriarchal, the matriarchs get plenty of airtime as well. For Peter, such women trusted in God and accepted the authority of their husbands. This is a fine line but points to Peter's sympathies with the married women of his time. Each woman must first trust God. You can't decide not to follow God because your husband doesn't want to do so. Women, your unbelieving husbands can't be your excuse not to become women of God! That being said, Peter's culture had strict codes concerning the relationship between spouses, and those were to be upheld for the sake of the church. I love that Sarah is mentioned here because she was feisty, and there were times when Abraham absolutely capitulated to her will. A close study of their marriage would indicate that it was a bit of a mess, but most married people know something of that kind of thing. What is noteworthy about Sarah? She called Abraham her "master," but he was not her "God."

> In the same way, husbands must give honor to your wives. Treat your wife with understanding as you live together. She may be weaker than you are, but she is your equal partner in God's gift of new life. Treat her as you should so your prayers will not be hindered. (1 Peter 3:7)

This short verse is for Christian husbands. Remember, the New Testament writers make no assumptions that they have authority over nonbelievers. Remember that the denotation of "weakness" for women means "in the eyes of Rome." The mention of equal partnership is "in the eyes of Christ." This is essentially the same argument Peter made concerning slaves who are Christians. Let's take this verse apart and then put it back together.

Christian Husbands

Honor your wife.

Offer understanding to your wife.

Live with your wife.

Treat her as an equal partner.

Treat her as a gift from God.

Realize you stand on equal ground before God.

Failure to do so will hinder your prayers.

As this very practical section wraps up, we might say that Peter instructs Christians to create a healthy subculture amidst a pagan culture. This subculture best serves the persecuted church if it looks normal from the outside and best honors Christ by being revolutionary on the inside. Now for some more advice in the form of one of my all-time favorite things: a list!

> Finally, all of you should be of one mind. Sympathize with each other. Love each other as brothers and sisters. Be tenderhearted and keep a humble attitude. Don't repay evil for evil. Don't retaliate with insults when people insult you. Instead, pay them back with a blessing. That is what God has called you to do, and he will grant you his blessing.
> (1 Peter 3:8–9)

There are two ways to view this material. First, we can say, "These are things Christians should be doing in the context of the church, and we'd best take a crack at them." Secondly, we can say, "These are clear features of a healthy and functional congregation." I would like to explore the latter trail since the first one seems to have everybody already on it. For our purposes, we will say, "In a healthy church, the people will . . ."

Further Instructions for Believers

Be of one mind.

Show empathy for one another.

Love one another (phileo).

Show compassion to one another.

Be humble.

Don't repay evil for evil.

Don't retaliate after an insult.

Bless those who curse you.

Those who heed these instructions will be blessed because of it. There is something about Bible-believing Christians this world will never understand. We believe our best lives are lived according to God's clear instruction . . . and instruction doesn't get any clearer than what we read in 1 Peter!

Questions for Discussion and Reflection

1. Spiritual beauty begins on the inside and works its way out. What are some qualities of someone who is spiritually beautiful?

2. How can you create a culture that is spiritually beautiful? In your church? At your work? In your relationships?

Enjoying Life and Seeing Happy Days

In May 2017 I published an anecdotal blog on happiness. I titled it "12 Things I See Happy People Do (That Unhappy People Do Not)" and attached a photo of me in my oldest Cardinals hat that was taken in downtown Memphis. The rest is a sort of history, and to date, 3,873,167 people have read the blog. Let me share it with you as we open.

> I have been thinking a lot about happiness of late, partially because so many people seem unhappy. I think that was my first epiphany upon entering the world of social media. People are unhappy, and there are a lot of them. Now don't get me wrong. We all know people who wouldn't be happy were they not unhappy, but I am not talking about them. We will just let them be. I am also not thinking theologically here (i.e., juxtaposing happiness and joy). Today I am going to err on the practical and pragmatic side of things. With that being said, let's get going.
>
> I think most people want to be happy. They are just not quite sure how to get there from their present location. Many people honestly believe that happiness is a lucky bounce, a

sunny disposition or favorable circumstances, but I disagree. Happiness is a choice. I believe that the best route to happiness is found by following the footsteps of those who have already arrived.

Here are my observations on the topic that have been formed by watching happy people for decades.

Focus on what you have and not on what you don't. Unhappy people are unthankful people. The practice of counting your blessings is a great start. Get out a legal pad and write down all the good things in your life. Often unhappiness sneaks in when we lose sight of all the good things in our life and become focused on one or two difficult things.

Question the sources of your expectations. Most unhappy people want things they don't have ... and they want them badly. Are these expectations realistic? Who is selling them to you? I hope not the media. Having a miserable existence because you are not living into a pipe dream is really tragic.

Be generous. Study after study has come to the same conclusion. Selfish people are miserable. Happy people give of their time and resources to a cause greater than themselves.

Remember, happiness is not a destination. The happiest people I know are those least conscious of their own happiness. Happiness is learning to enjoy the ride, not reaching your destination.

If you don't like your life, change it. Take control of your own life. Do you want to learn to play the piano? Take lessons! Do you regret not getting a college degree? Get one. Do you want to improve your spiritual life? Start going to church. There is really no one holding you back but you.

Slow down. You just can't smell the roses at a full sprint! If you, like me, are a workaholic type, build time into your Outlook to do nothing. Get a hobby. Enjoy your friends and family. Happy people have learned how to occasionally chill.

Realize that there are no shortcuts. If you were honestly disappointed that you didn't win the billion-dollar Power Ball, you are not getting it. Getting your education, working hard, putting in the hours, pursuing your dreams, saving, and giving are always in style.

Stop feeling entitled. No one owes you anything. Just assume you are not going to get any help, that you will receive no inheritance, and that no one is going to give you a break. Now go make your life happen! If anything else comes (and it probably will), it is all bonus!

Think significance. Significance is achieved by leaving the world better than you found it. People who feel their lives really matter are the happiest people of all!

Forgive. Forgiving those who have hurt you breaks their power over you. Forgiving yourself for your failures frees you for future success. Ask God to forgive you. Ask those you have hurt to forgive you. Make restitution where you can. Move on.

A great attitude is a choice, not a disposition. We can control our feelings, or we can be controlled by them. Happy people CHOOSE to have great attitudes.

Speak life. When you speak, choose words that uplift, encourage, and bring positive energy into every situation. My mom was right: "If you don't have something nice to say, you shouldn't say anything at all." People who speak life are like human air fresheners.

As you begin a new week, you have an opportunity to invest in your own happiness or to make yourself miserable. If you choose the former, you will make others happy as well. If you choose the latter . . . well, you know.

In our text this chapter, Peter surprisingly gives his persecuted readers some instruction on happiness! How to be happy. How to stay happy. How to find peace in the storm. How to keep peace in the storm. I don't think anyone saw this coming. Not only that, but he has to backtrack to Psalm 34:12–16 to get there!

Keep in mind that Peter is writing to persecuted Christians in Asia Minor. His big theme seems to be "Things are really tough and are probably going to get worse, so don't make things harder for yourselves than they have to be."

Let's review verses 8–9.

Finally, all of you should be of one mind. Sympathize with each other. Love each other as brothers and sisters. Be tenderhearted and keep a humble attitude. Don't repay evil for evil. Don't retaliate with insults when people insult you. Instead, pay them back with a blessing. That is what God has called you to do, and he will grant you his blessing.
(1 Peter 3:8–9)

Reviewing Instructions for Believers

Be of one mind. The imperative for unity within the church runs throughout the teachings of Jesus, Paul, and the New Testament in general. A unified church is an effective church. This points to the necessity of a mission statement. Early church leaders such as Peter dealt with things threatening the unity of the church with "extreme prejudice."

Show empathy for one another. This reflects less of a feeling than a deep emotional connection. Innumerable events have occurred in our nation in recent years that have caused pain to many of the people I know and love. I am often not fully able to comprehend the depths of their despair, but the Bible doesn't ask me to do that. I am asked to show empathy. I can rejoice with you, and I can hurt with you, not because I completely "get" you, but because we are connected through Christ Jesus.

Love one another (phileo). Love is to be the defining characteristic of the church and the lens by which we view one another and the world around us. To be sure, love nurtures, builds up, encourages, edifies, and exhorts. But love is not always affirmation. Love can sometimes come in the form of a rebuke if the basis of the rebuke is the well-being of the person receiving the rebuke, which also protects the overall mission of the church. The purpose of Christian love is to make us more like Christ, not to make us feel better about the sin in our lives.

Show compassion to one another. Compassion says, "I care about your suffering. There is pity in my heart for you. The pain in your life hurts me as well because I love you." And yet compassion, like love, is not always affirming. Sometimes the compassionate thing is to stop enabling bad behaviors, tell people the truth, and force someone to stand on their own two feet. "I care about you enough to be honest with you" is a decidedly Christian thing to say.

Be humble. Humility always holds two things above all: our total reliance upon God and our reliance upon one another. Humility is not a theological word for low self-esteem and self-loathing. It is confidently living in the power of the Holy Spirit. My single favorite Bible verse denoting humility is, "I can do everything through Christ, who gives me strength" (Philippians 4:13). In my own strength, I don't have much to offer. When I operate in Christ, watch out!

Don't repay evil for evil. Always take the high road. It is never crowded, and the view is always spectacular! Revenge is a pit with no bottom, and if you tread that path, what is good and noble in you will ultimately be destroyed.

Some years back Melissa bought the grandkids an ant farm. At first it was great, but then some of the indigenous ants began to mysteriously die amidst allegations of cannibalism. Melissa ordered more ants online (the source of all ants) and released the troops, and then things went really bad. The two armies established residence on each end of the farm, declaring war on one another, and our grandchildren witnessed global annihilation theory as one colony destroyed the other before turning on itself. The ants just couldn't find a place to stop hurting one another until there were no ants left to be hurt or to cause harm. There are only losers in wars like that . . .

Don't retaliate after an insult. Have you ever been on a walk on a country road in the summer and come upon some fresh, juicy roadkill? I don't know what you do, but I don't study it, try to estimate the time of death, do accident reconstruction, skin it for pelts, put police tape around the body, or call the county to send in the roadkill truck. I pinch my nose and just walk on by. Sometimes when you see a steaming hunk of "articulated stupid" lying in front of you, you just have to pinch your nose and walk on by. Let insults go. They will be out of sight soon enough, and their stench will soon be gone as well.

Bless those who curse you. If you are wondering where Peter heard this one, it was directly from Jesus. I learned long ago that it takes two enemies to have a war, so I am going to leave my detractors one enemy short of a war. We can't hate each other if I refuse to hate you. Only when we die to self and put full trust in God's Word can the nature of Christ Jesus resurrect within us.

Now we are ready to push on down the trail. As we have discovered, Peter's writing style is to make a point and then back it up with the Old Testament. Peter's quote to support what we have just explored comes from Psalm 34:12–16.

> For the Scriptures say, "If you want to enjoy life and see many happy days, keep your tongue from speaking evil and your lips from telling lies. Turn away from evil and do good. Search for peace, and work to maintain it."
> (1 Peter 3:10–11)

I believe life is a gift from God. I believe that babies have a right to life on either side of the womb, and cultures that rage against life rage against God. If I could say one thing to young people today, it would be that life is not a curse to be endured; it is a gift to be enjoyed. "Comfortably Numb" is a good Pink Floyd song, but it is a waste of the life God has given us. Jesus didn't come to make your life miserable. You could have been miserable without him. Jesus said in John 10:10, "I have come that [you] might have life, and have it to the full" (NIV). Next Peter gives us instruction for how to live full lives even in times of persecution:

How to Enjoy Life

Don't speak evil. This is speech with harmful intent. Speech of the flesh. Speech that does not glorify God. Carey Nieuwhof tweeted, "Expressing an opinion on everything cheapens your opinions on anything, including your area of expertise." For me as a pastor, opinions I give on things other than Christ weaken my witness for Christ. Peter would heartily concur. Think about all the times when things would have gone so much better if only you had kept your mouth shut. Clearly, the often-swiped Abraham Lincoln quote "It is better to be silent and be thought a fool than to speak and remove all doubt" applies here. There is a Southern saying that I often turn into a prayer: "Lord, please shut my mouth before anything else gets torn up."

Don't tell lies. This refers to untruths that come out of our mouths and implies a sinister nature or outcome. Again, this is a credibility issue. If Christians lie about some things, what makes you think they are not lying about Christ as well? The ancient Jews believed that words once spoken take on a life of their own. If you tell a lie in an age of social media, that thing can go from a spark to an uncontrollable wildfire in about thirty seconds. Peter is saying that you will be a lot happier in the long run if you tell the truth in the short run.

Turn from evil. You could argue that humans are born facing evil. We are turned the wrong way. In the Garden of Eden, Adam and Eve were created with their faces turned toward God. To sin, they had to intentionally turn away. Now because of sin, if we are to find God, we must turn toward God. It is not lost on me that the Greek word for "worship" is a compound word that denotes turning from sin and turning toward Christ. The hymn comes to mind: "Turn your eyes upon Jesus . . ."

Do good. This Greek word denotes goodness in every way. Good in thought, intent, motive, deed, and outcome. This is doing good when no one is looking, when nothing is to be gained, good for the sake of good. Good people enjoy life in a way that evil people cannot because we always see others through the eyes of who we are. The good see good in others.

Find peace. Media moguls have figured out that there is money to be made in keeping people radiating at high frequencies. From national news to cable news to the local weather, the big idea is simple: take away a person's sense of peace, and you can sell them stuff. We are conditioned to live in fear and summarily instructed through commercials in how to quell that fear. We used to know all about Pavlov's dogs and conditioned responses from psychology class, but now we are Pavlov's dogs. Take away our peace, and we buy stuff. In a fallen world, peace must be defined as the presence of God, rather than the absence of conflict. Though macro-peace will not be found until Jesus returns, inner peace is available to each of us right now. Find Jesus, and you will find peace.

Maintain peace. Peace is fragile. The Christian disciplines of prayer, corporate worship, Bible study, fellowship, service to others, witness, and tithes all work to maintain peace in our lives by keeping our lives ordered according to God. In a fallen world, Christians exhibiting peace in the midst of a storm will distinguish themselves and have a powerful witness.

> The eyes of the Lord watch over those who do right, and his ears are open to their prayers. But the Lord turns his face against those who do evil. (1 Peter 3:12)

God is watching over us when we walk in his ways. He is keeping an eye on us. Even in the most difficult of times, if we are turned toward God, we will never be alone. He will hear our prayers and will not only protect us but fight against those who work against God's work in us.

For Peter, the key to happiness is living in such a way as God's face is turned toward us, not against us. When God turns toward us and we turn toward God, a communion happens that we call worship. Worship is an interface in which we seek nothing but God. At that point of union, the supernatural work of God is accomplished in our lives. The greater the union, the greater the work. The more consistent the union, the more consistent the work. The deeper the union, the deeper the work. Worship is as good as life in this world gets.

Through worship, God heals, restores, renews, revives, and empowers us. Worship is a distinctly heavenly activity fully available to us on earth. I don't think we will come fully into union with God in this life. We have too much sin in each of us. But I do believe that heaven will be "full union" worship for eternity.

 ## Questions for Discussion and Reflection

1. What are one or two of the "12 Things I See Happy People Do (that unhappy people don't)" that you need to imitate?

2. What is one of the six ways to enjoy life that you would most benefit from focusing on? Why?

You Will Get Hit

First Peter addresses Christians in Asia Minor who are suffering waves of persecution from the Emperor Nero. Peter's argument has been singular: "Don't make things harder than they need to be." Peter implores Christians to live low-drama lives because there is no way to escape the cultural pushback accompanying the faith. He also implies that the ill-advised actions of any Christian will impact all Christians.

Imagine a group of kids playing in the woods. One finds a really cool ball hanging from a tree, has no idea what it is, decides to knock it down, and then starts poking it with a stick. This kid has no idea that he has just "stirred up a hornet's nest." When the hornets angrily emerge from the dislodged nest looking for vengeance, they will be most indiscriminate concerning whom they sting. Every kid playing in the woods may well get stung because of the actions of one kid who couldn't tell a hornet's nest from a piñata. Peter is telling his readers not to be that kid. "You go poking Caesar with a stick, and we will all pay the price for it."

> Now, who will want to harm you if you are eager to do good? But even if you suffer for doing what is right, God will reward you for it. So don't worry or be afraid of their threats. (1 Peter 3:13–14)

Last week I had a baseball workout with my three grandsons. Our theme was "Why you don't have to be afraid of the baseball." The answer is simple: "Because it is going to hit you! And when it hits you, it will hurt, but you will probably survive." Peter's logic is not dissimilar. Why don't Christians need to fear persecution? Because it is going to hit us, and though it may present unfair challenges or even take our earthly lives, our eternal souls will survive.

There are four big ideas offered to help us navigate persecution:

Four Big Ideas

1. Doing good things shrinks our target area.

2. Doing good things does not eliminate our target area.

3. Even if we are hit (persecuted), God will reward us.

4. There is no reason for worry or fear.

Three or four years back, American popular culture suddenly decided that traditional churches with biblical stands on human sexuality were haters of the worst sort. It was as though you went to bed one night a perfectly fine person and awoke the next day to discover you were a hater. At Christ Church we believe that Christian marriage is a monogamous, lifetime union between a man and a woman, and we believe in celibacy outside of marriage. These are positions we hold for those choosing to live within the bounds of the community of faith because we believe these to be in union with clear biblical teaching. Regardless of what the world says, these are not positions we hold out of hate. These are positions we hold in love. We want God's very best for all people, and we believe it is God who determines what is and what isn't sin, not us. We do not believe that unconditional love necessitates unconditional approval. We are going to treat everyone really well (whether they share our beliefs and practices or not), but we are not backing off the biblical Christian ethic. I believe that our best lives are lived doing things God's way. Period.

I can't tell you how many posts I read and messages I received during those years about how out of step we were and how awful we were, but our reputation in the community helped us. People have seen love, compassion, and good works coming from this church for decades, and that witness defended us against some of their slander. Theological progressives argue that traditional Christians holding our position on human sexuality are on the wrong side of history. Frankly, I don't care. I just want to be on the right side of God.

> Instead, you must worship Christ as Lord of your life. And if someone asks about your hope as a believer, always be ready to explain it. (1 Peter 3:15)

Instead of what? Worrying and living in fear concerning possible persecution! Instead of focusing our mind on worry, we are encouraged to focus on the worship of Jesus as the sole Lord of our lives. The reality is that you can't worry and worship. Worry is the absence of worship, and worship is the absence of worry. I can recall times in my life when worry threatened to overwhelm me. The only antidote was to worship, for it was only there that my mind shook free of the things consuming it.

I believe that worship is the cure for almost everything, but often we fail to properly engage it. You can't worship God *and* take your fears and anxieties into that space. There is no room for them there. You have to dump that stuff to get into the throne room. Through worship God provides peace, restoration, and healing as our hearts are lifted to him. My goal at this point of my faith walk is to abide in worship as much as possible. It is in the "God Zone" that we live our best lives. We are protected from evil, and we are freed to explore the heart of God. This is the zone where Jesus truly is not just our savior but our Lord. When we enter into worship, we are free!

Finally, Peter's church is encouraged to think about the content of their witness should they be asked. Why would someone ask? Because they see how well Christians hold up under persecution. Imagine that someone said to you, *"I notice you are different from everyone else. You work where everyone else does and have the same stressors, but you seem to have joy and peace. Why is that?"* What would you have to tell them? I want to suggest that the more thought you put into that now, the more effective your witness will be when the time comes. I think that the discipline of writing out a 250-word (one-page) testimony or a three-minute video testimony is a great place to begin this task. There are times that the Bible says to not worry about what to say concerning witnessing. This isn't one of them.

> But do this in a gentle and respectful way. Keep your conscience clear. Then if people speak against you, they will be ashamed when they see what a good life you live because you belong to Christ. Remember, it is better to suffer for doing good, if that is what God wants, than to suffer for doing wrong!
> (1 Peter 3:16–17)

How we say a thing is at least as important as what we say. People can't hear the right thing if it is presented the wrong way. Have you ever had a conversation with someone in which the essential substance was entirely missed due to the spirit of the delivery? This is why difficult conversations must never occur over email or text: if something can be taken wrongly, it will be. We should think about the way we say something every bit as much as we think about what we are going to say.

Let's divide our personal witness into content and spirit of delivery and see how it plays out. Many years ago I was on a No Greater Love evangelistic outreach to the Indianapolis 500. I had a young professional street preacher placed in my group who was trained by a legendary street preacher named Jed Smock. Back then there were a handful of these street/campus preacher guys around, and most of them were some combination of evangelism, apologetics, and public entertainment. This included the legendary Holy Hubert Lindsey who wore the vest of a Hell's Angels gang member he had led to Christ. A favorite quip was the crowd once asking, "God made marijuana, why don't you smoke it?" and Holy Hubert replying, "God made poison ivy, why don't you chew it?" You get the idea. Most of these guys were playful, witty, and entertaining, but the guy in my group was just plain mean. When it was his turn to take the microphone, he castigated everyone within the sound of his voice in a most abrasive manner. More than a few people in the crowd were fired up and pushed in hard. All that stood between him and the quickly forming mob was my group of about eight or ten guys who were looking to me for instruction on what to do. I told them, "I am not going to get beat up because this guy is an idiot. Either God will protect him or he won't." We left. When we operate in the flesh, we are on our own. When we share faith, we must never allow the manner with which we say a thing to diminish what we are saying.

How should we offer our witness?

 ## How to Witness in Difficult Times

Gently. Gentle means that a thing has the capacity to do harm or to destroy but chooses not to do so. By this definition a bear can be gentle. A hamster cannot. A gentle witness is a witness in which we are committed to doing no harm. We might call it a "tender witness."

Respectfully. Managing our tone of voice, not being condescending, listening and not talking the whole time, giving serious consideration to questions, and simply being polite are ways that we show respect to others.

With a clear conscience. This means not having things to regret when the interchange is completed. You don't want to share your faith and then think, "I wish I had said this," or "I shouldn't have said that." That is why Peter tells us to put some time into our testimony.

I am not an avid deer hunter despite the fact that I have strong enthusiasm around our annual deer hunting weekends. My wife Melissa and son Zec are the true hunters in the family, and they will both tell you one thing. You often get only one shot, and it can all happen before you know it. Last year Melissa and Zec decided to walk into a hunting area together. Before they could even begin to unpack Melissa's stuff, a big buck appeared in front of them. Though they were startled, their guns were loaded. Melissa shot. Zec shot. Melissa turned to Zec and said, "What in the world just happened?" What happened is that deer's head will spend the next few decades mounted to our cabin wall above the fireplace. The moral of the story is you have to be ready because you never know when the opportunity will present itself. Faith sharing is a lot like that. Sometimes you get only one shot, so you had best be ready.

Peter is fully aware that being a witness for Christ in a time of persecution will lead to trouble. It is inevitable. Some will be thrown out of their families, some will become pariahs, some will lose their jobs, and a handful will lose their lives. He wants to make sure that when the "ball hits" this church, it will be because they are wisely sharing their faith under the influence of the Holy Spirit and not because they can't tell a hornet's nest from a piñata.

Now, as we have become accustomed to seeing Peter do, he follows his latest set of practical instructions with some theological underpinnings in what we might call "A Theology of the Persecuted."

> Christ suffered for our sins once for all time. He never sinned, but he died for sinners to bring you safely home to God. He suffered physical death, but he was raised to life in the Spirit. (1 Peter 3:18)

Theology for the Persecuted

The cross was "one time for all time."

Jesus never sinned. In Judaism a lamb without "spot or blemish" was sacrificed annually on the Day of Atonement for the sins of the people. In Christianity the sacrifice of Jesus was a once-and-for-all cure from sin. Jesus was the perfect lamb, and the sacrifice was "once-and-for-all time."

Jesus died to bring sinners "safely home to God."

Jesus died physically. Jesus was not dead(ish) on the cross. He died.

Jesus arose to life. Jesus was not alive(ish) after the resurrection. He was alive.

What did Jesus do after the resurrection?

> So he went and preached to the spirits in prison—those who disobeyed God long ago when God waited patiently while Noah was building his boat. Only eight people were saved from drowning in that terrible flood. And that water is a picture of baptism, which now saves you, not by removing dirt from your body, but as a response to God from a clean conscience. It is effective because of the resurrection of Jesus Christ. (1 Peter 3:19–21)

This passage is functionally impossible to unravel, but at its heart it makes claim to the nature of the ministry of Christ and to baptism as a seal of that ministry. Let's unpack what we can get out of the suitcase.

History has been described as a guitar string with one end inserted into creation and the other tied to the Second Coming of Christ. Anywhere you pluck on the string sends reverberations in every direction. So too was the life, death, and resurrection of Jesus Christ. In ways we cannot begin to comprehend, the work of Christ reached far back into history to set captives free.

The Genesis flood was a baptism of death bringing destruction to the wicked. Jewish purifications were a baptism of the body to wash off the dirt. Christian baptism is a death to self (going under) and a resurrection to new life (coming up). It is God's "official seal" upon us.

To sum things up, it appears that after the resurrection, Jesus ran down Satan, settled some old scores, cleaned up some of the mess he had made, and gave him a butt whooping. Beyond that, we will have to play the "That's What It Says and Just Move On" card.

> Now Christ has gone to heaven. He is seated in the place of honor next to God, and all the angels and authorities and powers accept his authority. (1 Peter 3:22)

This can be summed up in the phrase "Jesus is Lord." At this time in the Roman Empire, residents of Asia Minor were expected to annually take a pinch of incense before a magistrate and declare, "Caesar is Lord." This meant that they subjected themselves totally and completely to the dominion of the emperor. Not shockingly, Christians took a "hard pass" and sometimes defiantly declared, "Jesus is Lord." Peter is reminding his persecuted church that Jesus has everything in his control.

Kurt Warner was the quarterback of the "Greatest Show on Turf" back before the Rams went extinct in St. Louis. When the Rams let Warner go, my affections followed him to the Giants and later to the Arizona Cardinals where he made his comeback. When the Cardinals played a late Sunday afternoon game and I had meetings at church all day, I would tape the game and hope that no one told me the score before I got home from church. One such Sunday I almost made it to my car before someone yelled, "Cardinals won!" Terrible. After some debate I watched my recorded game anyway and was surprised to find that the Cardinals were losing for most of the game. But regardless of the score, there was no anxiety in me (like there would be had I been watching live) . . . because I already knew the outcome of the game. I didn't have to be stressed, despite the score, because I knew the Cardinals had already won!

Here is the deal: Jesus wins. Because we know that, we don't have to live in fear and anxiety regardless of the trials and tribulations that may be bearing down upon us . . . because the outcome has already been determined.

 ## Questions for Discussion and Reflection

1. Do you struggle with focusing on worry? Do you also have a lack of worship in your life? How can you change your pattern or help someone else?

2. Use the space given and write a short witness/testimony on your life. How has God changed you? Be gentle, respectful, and have a clear conscience.

No Time for Games

Imagine this. It's not so hard. Orthodox Christianity has been outlawed by the state. Quoting the Bible is officially hate speech, and offenders are subject to civil law. Bible-believing Christians are attacked on media outlets and social media platforms, becoming public pariahs. Churches meet knowing that governmental officials are listening to every word, eager to pounce on the slightest inflection that does not align with their narrative. Pastors are fined for anything they say not aligned with the prevailing narrative. And then things relax.

Then comes the next wave. Conservative pastors are arrested and interrogated as cult leaders, churches not holding a governmental line lose tax-exempt status, and anyone contributing financially to a forbidden church is placed on a watch list. Churches begin to close. And then things relax.

Then comes the next wave. Christians are driven from their professions, publicly slandered, and pushed to the edges of society. Pastors are increasingly jailed, church leaders are routinely arrested and interrogated, church assets are frozen, and influential conservative Christian leaders are declared enemies of the state. And then things relax.

Then comes the next wave. High-profile Christian leaders are martyred, church assets are seized, and the bank accounts of church members are frozen unless they renounce their faith in Christ. Churches go underground, and Christians communicate off the grid. And then things relax. And then comes the next wave.

Could such things happen today? They already do. The *World Watch List* reports that in 2020 over 340 million Christians around the world experienced high levels of persecution; 4,761 Christians were killed for their faith; 4,488 church buildings were attacked and 1710 members abducted; and 4,277 believers were detained without trial, arrested, or imprisoned. That means seven Christians a day forfeited their lives for their faith. Systemic oppression is a reality for about one in eight Christians worldwide. Such intense waves of persecution were the reality of many of the Christians living in Asia Minor to whom Peter writes. In times like these there was no time for games.

> So then, since Christ suffered physical pain, you must arm yourselves with the same attitude he had, and be ready to suffer, too. For if you have suffered physically for Christ, you have finished with sin. You won't spend the rest of your lives chasing your own desires, but you will be anxious to do the will of God. (1 Peter 4:1–2)

Peter's point is unambiguous. To share in Christ's glory, you will have to share in Christ's suffering. This is no metaphor. This is reality. Just as Christ sacrificed his life for us, his followers must be prepared to sacrifice their lives for him. There is no way around this. You can't straddle the fence between the values of God and the things of this world. For almost all of my life, American Christians have lived with nothing that could be construed as persecution at a New Testament level. Then things got harder, not historically hard, but harder nonetheless. Like many of the Gentile Christians to whom Peter wrote, we were not used to pushback of any kind concerning our faith. Seemingly overnight we had to choose between biblical values or the values of an increasingly godless culture. Many former church attenders chose the latter when things got hard. The drop in pre-pandemic worship attendance across the nation bears witness to this reality. The pandemic only accelerated what was already happening. Like Joshua 24:15 says, we were each forced to "choose today whom you will serve," and those who declared, "As for me and my family, we will serve the Lord" have been thrust into a movement of the Holy Spirit that does not occur apart from persecution.

To hunger for the things of God means being finished with the things of this world. To quote Jesus, "No one can serve two masters" (Matthew 6:24). To embrace God is to reject sin. To embrace sin is to reject God. Embracing the will of God for our lives means to reject the desires of our nature apart from God. Embracing the holy means to reject the profane. In times of spiritual revival, we look forward to disciplines such as prayer, worship, Bible study, giving, witness, and service as the world looks to a "night on the town." To revisit our metaphor of baptism, we die to the sin that dwells in each of us, and we are resurrected to a new life in Christ Jesus. That new life does not contain the contents of the dead one.

> You have had enough in the past of the evil things that godless people enjoy—their immorality and lust, their feasting and drunkenness and wild parties, and their terrible worship of idols.
> (1 Peter 4:3)

Let me paraphrase. Haven't you already wasted enough of your life on things that don't matter? The list of profane things that Peter offers were woven into the fabric of his world. These are common, not uncommon, things. Peter's point is that these common practices for non-believers have no place in the lives of believers or in the church. Peter is calling his audience into a life of individual and collective holiness, a life set apart for a special purpose.

Let's take a moment to see what we can learn about things common to a fallen world that have no place in the church.

Profane Things

Immorality. Clear teaching about human sexuality protects both the people and the witness of the church. At our church we believe Christian marriage is a monogamous, lifetime union between a man and a woman, and we believe in celibacy outside of marriage. When this is our standard, church becomes a safe place where we can live as brothers and sisters in Christ.

Lust. This is obsessively desiring what is not yours to have. The commandment "Thou shall not covet" gets at the heart of it.

Feasting. This refers to gluttony, places where people meet to overeat. I have noted over the years that people tend to rail against sins that don't represent a personal temptation to them. Therefore, we often make the sins we are least dispositioned to commit the worst sins of all.

Drunkenness. I don't drink, but I cannot build a decisive biblical case for my position. However, the Bible never waivers on its condemnation of drunkenness. Bad things happen when people are drunk. Always have. Always will.

Wild parties. The Romans were a social lot and tried to keep some form of propriety, but things often got out of hand, even by pagan standards. The fact that the Emperor Nero and the upper classes trying to gain his favor often practiced compulsive moral debauchery didn't help. Peter did not expect Nero to act like a Christian, but he clearly expected Christians not to act like Nero.

Worship of idols. Polytheism (worship of many gods) was central to Greco-Roman life and completely antithetical to Judeo-Christian life. Worship of the gods was a straight-up industry in the Roman Empire. From the construction of elaborate pagan temples to the conduct of their cultic practice to the making, sale, and distribution of idols, polytheism was an economic engine. Clearly, some of the persecution aimed at Christians was that their belief in one God hurt business. I never get the feeling that most first-century Romans believed as fervently in Zeus as the Bronze Age Canaanites believed in Baal, but there were still significant economic interests to protect.

> Of course, your former friends are surprised when you no longer plunge into the flood of wild and destructive things they do. So they slander you. (1 Peter 4:4)

Christianity shares two unique tenets of Judaism that vastly differentiated them from the prevailing culture of their day. First is a belief in one God and that all other gods are false gods. There is not a lot of negotiating room here. Secondly, Jews, and later Christians, represented a shift from pagan religion and "footloose and fancy free" immorality to religion and immutable morality based in unchanging Scripture. While many pagan temples raised money through sacred prostitution (later replaced by bake sales), Judaism brought something very different. In the Ten Commandments, faith and morality were linked. It was the shockingly countercultural morality of the members of the early church that got the attention of the Roman world. Like the Jews before them, Christians were not willing to assimilate into Hellenistic culture, and what the world doesn't understand, the world attacks.

> But remember that they will have to face God, who stands ready to judge everyone, both the living and the dead. That is why the Good News was preached to those who are now dead—so although they were destined to die like all people, they now live forever with God in the Spirit. (1 Peter 4:5–6)

This door can swing one of two ways. Peter may be trying to comfort the members of the early churches whose friends had turned on them by reminding them that those former friends will have to face God someday. That would be like a former friend saying, "Since you became a Christian, you think you are better than all of us," and you reply, "At least I won't burn in an eternal hell." It may be true, but it behooved Peter's audience to do better than that in terms of their relationships with their pagan neighbors.

Yet I think this door swings the other way. We are being asked to remember that apart from Christ our unbelieving friends and family will someday stand in final judgment. A good thing for believers will be a tragic thing for non-believers. It's imperative to share our faith boldly while we still can because eternity is at stake.

The final idea about preaching to the dead continues the difficult section we discussed previously and reminds us why keeping a "Just Move On" card handy is always a good idea.

> The end of the world is coming soon. Therefore, be earnest and disciplined in your prayers. Most important of all, continue to show deep love for each other, for love covers a multitude of sins. Cheerfully share your home with those who need a meal or a place to stay. (1 Peter 4:7–9)

The Bible is clear that this earth comes with a shelf life. So how do we make the most of the time that has been given to us?

Redeeming Our Time

Be earnest in prayer. The Greek word translated "earnest" is a compound word that points to an intentional process of "guarding your mind." This is ingesting the good and keeping out the bad. Being earnest in prayer is preserving the relationship we have with God by being intentional concerning what goes into our minds.

Be serious in prayer.

This second thought on prayer literally means to be sober. This is actually closer to what we think of when Peter asks us to "be earnest." It is praying with your game face on.

Show deep love for one another. When Melissa and I first married, I took an entry-level teaching job at North Clay Jr. High in Louisville, Illinois. We lived in a cottage on Sailor Springs Road just above the Little Wabash River bottom. I remember our first big argument. The irresistible force hit the immovable object, and I was out of there. I fired up the engine of our blue Pontiac LeMans, stuck in a Boston 8-track, and was ready to leave. By the time I got to the river forty-five seconds later, I realized I had no place to go. I did a U-turn, went back home, and engaged in the hard work of loving. Deep love does not mean agreeing on everything. It is an honest love that stays at the table.

Cheerfully offer hospitality. A persecuted church requires an upbeat community in ways that the unscathed church does not. Oppressed churches don't "fuss and spit" over trivial things. They pull together. What is the nature of that community? Cheerfulness and genuine hospitality. Who doesn't want to be a part of a church like that?

Since following Christ involves wholesale change that will put you at odds with former aspects of your life, the serious Christian needs the love and support of the community. One of the true concerns I have with modern Christianity is the false narrative that what you believe and how you live are not connected. This is a problem that goes back to the early formation of Christian practice. You might say it is a "burning problem."

My dad tells a story about a woman he encountered on the square in Pinckneyville, Illinois, in the very early seventies. He saw her first and noticed that she was smoking a cigarette, or as my grandsons call it, a heat rod. Seeing her pastor approaching, she tucked the burning cigarette under her arm to conceal it. Dad, being Dad, just stood there chatting until the woman could stand the pain no longer and had to choose between coming clean and a hole burned into her armpit.

What interests me is that in the early 1970s, there was a clear understanding of how a Christian lived as opposed to how non-believers lived. I think that shared understanding is largely gone. In fact, these days the woman may well have taken a selfie with the cigarette in her mouth standing next to Dad and posted it on social media. There seems to be little linkage between what people believe and how they act. I don't think we are better for it.

I was raised in a conservative Christian culture. The circle of people closely surrounding my family treated each other well. They did not drink, take drugs, or use bad language, with the exception of a couple of uncles. No one even smoked cigarettes. You may say, "You were a kid, and they were probably all just hypocrites." Possibly, but I don't think so. I would have known that long before now. I am convinced that I was raised in the company of good Christian people, and even if it rendered me a bit judgmental in my early years, a solid moral foundation is something you can build a friendship, a marriage, a family, a career, and a life upon.

Back in those days, there were clear moral expectations concerning how a Christian behaved. I have watched those expectations erode in my own lifetime. Christianity has eroded with them. Are some Christians judgmental legalists and modern Pharisees? Without a doubt, but you can't throw out biblical morality because some traditions get all hateful about it. Being loving and being holy are not mutually exclusive realms of existence. They are two sides of the same coin. The contemporary notion that you can't stand both in biblical truth and Christian love is a lie forged in the pits of hell.

After we encounter Jesus, his parting words to us will always be "go and sin no more," never "as you were." To be a Christ follower in the Roman Empire meant to embrace a lifestyle that stood apart from the norms of the day. Though Jewish Christians were never a part of the pervasive pagan culture, most Gentile converts were. There was no judgment offered as Gentile unbelievers explored the Christian faith, but they fully understood that if they embraced Christ, there were expectations that came with it. If you one day wanted to be a church leader, those expectations became even more stringent. Those formally becoming a part of the early church were expected not only to change their beliefs but to change their ways.

 ## Questions for Discussion and Reflection

1. Are you willing to share in Christ's suffering just as much as His glory?

2. Are you making the most of the time God gives you? Write a prayer that is earnest, serious, and shows love.

Team Jesus

When I was a kid, you changed channels by walking up to the TV and manually rotating a plastic knob. When the knob broke, which it did, you turned channels with a pair of pliers. At our house there were only three regular channels and PBS, meaning there were three channels. The weird thing is that out of those channels, we always found something good to watch. Now that we have eight hundred channels, the only good stuff is the exact same stuff that was on back then . . . and sports. "The more channels you have, the less there is to watch."

We knew no such things as reality shows back then. Most people considered their regular lives to be all the reality they could stand, but there were plenty of private eye and cop shows. One of my favorites was *Starsky and Hutch.* They were cool undercover cops who drove a 1976 red Ford Grand Torino with an iconic white stripe. I always thought that if I were a cop, I would want to be an undercover cop. When *Miami Vice* later came out, I was positive. Going undercover made a good basis for a cop show, but "going undercover" is the wrong idea for people of faith. Too many Christians want to live "Undercover Christianity." We want to look like everyone else, act like everyone else, think like everyone else, have the same values as everyone else, and yet have a profoundly different destination for eternity. 1 Peter reminds us that we don't get that piece. Jesus said in Matthew 10:33 that if we deny him before people, he will deny us before the Father. To be a Christian in a fallen world is to stand up, stand out, and stand tall for Jesus . . . and sometimes to stand alone . . . even if it costs us everything, and the Bible makes no guarantees that it won't.

As we continue our journey, Peter shifts from the character of Christians to the ministries of Christians. Not so long ago, I asked my social media community to rate themselves on a scale of one to ten concerning whether they have a clear sense of purpose. What I noted was that very few people were in the middle. Most of the people responding either had a strong sense of purpose or didn't have much of one at all. For me, finding purpose has everything to do with discovering your gifts, developing them, and putting them into play in the context of the church! It is all about being a contributing part of Team Jesus!

I am a bit of a historian concerning baseball. When the balls began to get harder so players other than Babe Ruth could hit home runs, baseball mitts, which originally looked like leather oven mitts, began to morph into baseball gloves. First, they sewed on a pocket, and then things progressed from there.

Today ball gloves are highly specialized tools to aid players on the defensive side of baseball. A catcher's mitt is round, a first baseman's mitt is huge with one rounded side, an outfielder's glove may be the size of a shovel, and infielder's gloves are small for getting the ball quickly in and out. The differing gloves are designed for players playing different positions and are formed uniquely to aid that player. Employing different gloves helps the team. Gloves are "equipment." They equip players to be successful parts of the team.

> God has given each of you a gift from his great variety
> of spiritual gifts. Use them well to serve one another.
> (1 Peter 4:10)

The image I have here is a baseball coach with a whole bunch of ball gloves. As the players pass by, the coach gives them the specific piece of equipment that best suits them and will best help the team. His instruction is, "Break this thing in and learn to use it well because the better you are, the better we are."

When I think of spiritual gifts, I am reminded that there are clearly gifts that are higher profile than others. One of the things people with lower-profile gifts often struggle with is thinking they are not gifted at all. Peter challenges this way of thinking by declaring that God has given "each of you" a gift. He gives you the gifts he wants you to have that best suit the contributions to the Kingdom you are called to make. This refers to the people in the churches he leads and all who will ever claim the name of Christ. How do I know you are gifted? "The Bible tells me so!" What is the purpose of gifts? To make the church more effective in carrying on the ministry of Jesus Christ until his return.

In the same way, the Holy Spirit gives us different gifts to aid us in the service of God, the church, and one another. As an example of the gift spectrum, Peter offers one high-profile gift and juxtaposes it with one lower-profile gift to make the point that all gifts are essential to the work of the church. We are called to learn to use them well!

> Whoever speaks must do so as one speaking the very words of God. (1 Peter 4:11a)

Effectively communicating the gospel has always been an "upfront" gift in the church. Preachers and teachers are often the "faces" of a church. They are who most people see. I may be the "face" of Christ Church, but all I am doing is using the gift that God gave me obediently and to the best of my ability. Chief Speaker is a role God has given me on this team, and despite its high visibility, it is no more or less important than other roles. No matter how good a pitcher may be, the other eight players are absolutely essential for a baseball team.

Peter's imperative is to speak as though God himself were speaking through us. This is a grave responsibility that must not be taken lightly. It is so grave that specific criteria are outlined in the New Testament for those who play that position. In the pagan world, oracles were humans believed to be "possessed" by supernatural powers. Their gods literally spoke through them. There was a lot of showmanship and drama with it, but that was the basic idea. We shouldn't think of preaching and teaching in the same way, but we do need to re-emphasize that the goal is for God's voice to be heard. I preach and teach the Bible. Period. I believe God most accurately, often, and clearly communicates with us through the Bible, and God never speaks in ways that contradict the clear and consistent teachings of Holy Scripture. My task is to present God's Word to God's people, try to get out of the way, and trust the Holy Spirit to do the rest.

> Do you have the gift of helping others? Do it with all the strength and energy that God supplies. (1 Peter 4:11b)

Unlike speaking, where few people are highly gifted, helping is something we can all do. Peter states that some in the church have been particularly gifted to help. Helping is doing what needs to be done. It has as much to do with availability as ability. I read a post on social media this week in which a pastor cautioned Christians not to mistake work in the church for a relationship with Christ. My immediate thought was, "I suppose this could be a problem for 10 percent of any church, but the problem of the 90 percent is that they don't do anything at all!" A church our size could not operate without an army of people volunteering, or as Peter would say, serving. There is an incredible claim made here. If we will answer God's call to help, God will give us supernatural measures of strength and energy. Volunteering in your own power and with your own abilities may well wear you out or even burn you out, but helping under the influence of the Holy Spirit will actually increase your energy and stamina.

> Then everything you do will bring glory to God through Jesus Christ. All glory and power to him forever and ever! Amen. (1 Peter 4:11c)

No matter how good a pitcher is, he can't record a single out on his own. The best of pitchers still stands in need of the other players. You may counter that a pitcher could just strike everyone out, but unless a catcher catches the ball, the out is not recorded. Peter reminds everyone on the team that they are gifted, appreciated, and essential to the work of the church.

So what is the Christian progression concerning giftedness? Peter has given us five things from verses 10 and 11:

Progression of Giftedness

Receive your gifts. Gifts come from the Holy Spirit.

Identify your gifts. Where do you see God using you?

Develop your gifts. Our potential is God's gift to us; our performance is our gift to God. Gifts must be developed.

Give God your all. "If you are going to be a bear, be a Grizzly."

Glorify God with your gifts. Make pleasing, glorifying, and being obedient to God your endgame!

Dear friends, don't be surprised at the fiery trials you are going through, as if something strange were happening to you. (1 Peter 4:12)

The only thing this fallen world knows to do with something "not normal" to its values is to persecute it, for righteousness threatens the very foundations of sin. For years I tried to define the word "normal," and then I discovered the subjective definition that applies to us all objectively: normal is that and those most like me. But some years ago Melissa threatened my whole theory when she said, "Shane, you are just not normal."

A couple of weeks later, I attended a Cardinals game and had the opportunity to be on the field before the game. I stood there while the final field preparations were going on and the players were just starting to gather around. About that time an errant baseball rolled my way and stopped at my feet. The Cardinals guide smiled and said to me, "Go ahead and pick up your souvenir." I immediately thought, "If I pick this ball up, I will have to carry it around the whole game." I told him "no thanks" and let it lie. Then it hit me. That's not normal! Melissa was right. I am not normal.

If you are a Jesus follower, you are not normal either, and you are certainly not undercover. In fact, you have been given a unique gift set that God expects you to identify, develop, and put into play for Team Jesus. When we all submit to the manager, find the right positions, learn to use our equipment, and give of our very best, the church thrives, and when the church thrives, the devil pushes back. At that point it is not a matter of "if" persecution will come but "when." A persecuted church like the one to whom Peter writes does not have the luxury of offering comfort and quarter to undercover Christians. The stakes are too high. We must boldly wear the Team Jesus uniform, or we will be driven off the field altogether.

Questions for Discussion and Reflection

1. Do you know your Spiritual Gift? How are you using it for the Lord and in your church?

2. Are you spending time developing your Spiritual Gift? What can you do to learn more about using your gift to please God?

 # Holding Steady

Sometimes holding steady in challenging times can be the most difficult thing in the world to do. Often, when the storms are raging, we want to "do something," but sometimes holding steady is precisely the right thing to do. Some years back I heard an anecdotal statistic that 85 percent of all crises are rectified in forty-eight hours with or without intervention. I think that roughly holds true in my life and ministry as well. I can't tell you how many times my first reaction was the wrong reaction, and by holding steady I saved me and everyone around me a whole lot of time, effort, energy, and emotional turmoil. On the other hand, I can't tell you how many times my first reaction was the wrong reaction, and by failing to hold steady, I cost me and everyone around me a whole lot of time, effort, energy, and emotional turmoil. Often in my life and ministry, I have to tell myself time and time again to hold course, not panic, and remember that most storms blow over soon enough.

Peter's churches in Asia Minor were being hit by Hurricane Nero, and they weren't through the worst of it by a long shot. His advice to the churches of Asia Minor to whom he writes is to anticipate the storms, do your best to prepare for the storms, and then hold steady. For Peter, who may well have been martyred within a year or two of this writing, life storms for people of faith are inevitable. The only thing we can control is how we react to them.

> Dear friends, don't be surprised at the fiery trials you are going through, as if something strange were happening to you. (1 Peter 4:12)

The rhetorical use of fire concerning persecution fascinates me. It is a two-edged sword. Fire can be destructive or cleansing. The same fire that destroys wood purifies gold. The idea seems to be that the fiery persecution Satan inflicts to destroy us can be used by God to purify us. When people come on staff here, one of the first things for which they must prepare is having the target on their backs increase exponentially. There will be pushback, there will be difficult situations, and there will be persecution. My prayer is always that God would keep our hearts soft and our hides thick. Jewish Christians had suffered anti-Semitism from Rome in greater or lesser degrees for centuries. As a people, they had developed thick hides. The new Gentile Christians were not so seasoned. Persecution was an unfamiliar storm, and many were tempted to abandon ship to escape the pain that went with it.

One of the things I teach my grandsons in baseball is never to turn one error into two. If you don't cleanly catch a ground ball, don't pick it up so full of adrenaline that you throw the ball away. I tell them to "put the ball in their pocket." Or, in non-baseball speak, hold steady.

One of my tasks here is to spiritually prepare people for the inevitable difficult times in life. This keeps one storm from turning into two. Let me explain. Bad stuff is going to happen to good people in a fallen world. People are going to suffer illness, relational challenges, financial difficulties, emotional issues, and more. Spiritually, people are going to have times of discouragement, doubt, persecution, frustration, and more. My pastoral goal when your storm hits is to make sure your current crisis does not also become a theological crisis. I want to keep one storm from turning into two.

When I was in seminary, a classmate and fellow Southern Illinoian named Bob Cooley was killed in an automobile accident. It shook me to my core. When I got to sorting things out, it occurred to me that there were not one but two crises going on inside of me. First, I had lost a friend and colleague. Second, I had to sort out what I believed to be true about God in this tragic situation. The term "personal theology" simply means "what we believe to be true about God." At first, it consists primarily of what we have been told, but in time it either becomes our own or fades away. Our personal theology is built through reason, our understanding of Scripture, the religious tradition in which we place ourselves, and the crunch of real life.

When I was a student at SIU-Carbondale, there was an annual cardboard boat regalia, in which teams of students would build a cardboard boat and then attempt to paddle it across a lake on campus. A given boat may have a sleek design and be a thing of artistic beauty, but it is not until that boat is placed in the water that it can be established whether or not it will float! Tragedy like the one I experienced in seminary forces our theological boats into the water. Let me share five planks from my personal theology that always manage to float even in troubled water.

My Personal Theology in the Storms

God is good! The Bible says every good and perfect gift comes from God. The love we shared with those no longer with us and the impact they made upon our lives is clear evidence of God's love for us.

Bad things happen. Genesis tells us of how sin entered the world. Proverbs reminds us that it rains on the just and the unjust. Our faith in God is not an escape hatch that keeps pain away; it is a constant source of strength and hope as we live in a fallen world.

God is with us. God never leaves us, never forsakes us, and weeps with us during the most difficult times of life. The promises of God never have to do with avoiding difficulty; they have to do with presence through those hard times.

Sunday is coming. Each Sunday people of faith gather together to celebrate an empty tomb! When we worship, we are reminded that the gospel message is bigger than us, Christ is risen, and we are swallowed up in the glory of the thing.

Life goes on. Life will never again be the same for those affected by tragedy, but life does go on. Jesus was asked to wrap up the whole of the Law, and he replied that we are to love God and love one another. We cannot reverse the effects of tragedy, but we can choose to love rather than hate, celebrate life even as we mourn a death, and realize heaven awaits those who know Christ.

For me, every time a storm hits, and I once again place my boat in the water, is a time of revelation. I have learned to keep what floats and replace the things that sink with more buoyant things. Having a buoyant and watertight personal theology does not keep us from "the valley of the shadow of death," nor does it answer all of our questions, but it does keep tragedy from becoming an obstacle in our relationship with God. God feels our hurt, God can handle our pain, and

God loves us more than we could ever hope or imagine. Of these things we can be sure. Every difficult thing I have experienced in my life has rendered my cardboard boat better and stronger. The same fire that destroys also purifies.

> Instead, be very glad—for these trials make you partners with Christ in his suffering, so that you will have the wonderful joy of seeing his glory when it is revealed to all the world. If you are insulted because you bear the name of Christ, you will be blessed, for the glorious Spirit of God rests upon you. (1 Peter 4:13–14)

Here we have that upside-down gospel in which we are asked to respond to negative stimuli in counterintuitive ways. Peter states we should be glad when persecution comes our way. Why?

Persecution Positives

Partnership. We will not share in Christ's victory until we share in his suffering. Good Friday has to precede Easter. Why would Olympic athletes think they would not have to train? Why would we think that soldiers would not have to fight, and firemen and policemen would not have to protect? If we are true followers of the one who was crucified and suffered, why would we think that we will not suffer? In suffering we are brought into partnership with Christ.

Glory Sharing. The kind of glory described here is a future glory. There is something about the Olympics that always gets to me. When an American athlete is on the gold medal stand hearing the national anthem with tears in their eyes, my eyes well up with theirs. They share their glory with an entire country, and the hundreds of thousands of hours of training, blood, sweat, and tears have converged in one incredible moment of triumph that is bigger than anything else they will ever do, and the moment is so large it must be shared. One day we hear God say, "Well done, good and faithful servant." The national anthem of heaven will play in a place where the podiums are made of gold and Spirit winds blow our hair, and the glory of God will illuminate our face. And all who are, were, and are to come will share in that glory with us. You can hang on in the most violent storm when you know the story ends like that!

Glory Carrying. This kind of glory has Old Testament roots in a Hebrew word called *shekinah*. This was the kind of tangible, visible glory that filled the Tabernacle, that rested on the face of Moses when he came down the mountain, and that settled upon the apostle Stephen when he was being stoned. I have seen this kind of glory overtake the saints on their deathbeds as their spirits charged into heaven and left their withered bodies behind. I have felt it brush me when I am preaching, I have seen it in the faces of saintly people, and we are marinated in it when worship takes us from where we are to the plane where angels dance. There is such a thing as glory!

> If you suffer, however, it must not be for murder, stealing, making trouble, or prying into other people's affairs. But it is no shame to suffer for being a Christian. Praise God for the privilege of being called by his name!
> (1 Peter 4:15–16)

As Peter often does in this book, he gives us a peek at the Promised Land for inspirational purposes and then whisks us back to the battlefront. I draw a sharp delineation here between the causes of suffering. Christians who suffer for doing good bring glory to God. Christians who suffer for doing evil defame the name of God. The advice given here is, "Don't make things worse for yourselves by being a criminal, stirring up trouble, or not staying in your lane." This is a consistent theme for Peter: "Persecution is inevitable. Don't make things worse for all of us . . ."

It seems that the name "Christian" was originally used by critics of Christianity. They took a largely undefined word and filled it full of nefarious meanings such as being murderous, stealing, rousing the rabble, and being generally meddlesome. It is a political tactic we often see today. Take a word that no one is quite sure how to define such as "evangelical" and then fill it full of false definition. Peter wants to ensure that if Christians are to be arrested, it will be only for their unwavering faith in Christ. He argues that we best reject the false cultural narrative by collectively living lives that disprove it every single day.

> For the time has come for judgment, and it must begin with God's household. And if judgment begins with us, what terrible fate awaits those who have never obeyed God's Good News? And also, "If the righteous are barely saved, what will happen to godless sinners?" (1 Peter 4:17–18)

There has always been a strong belief in the Judeo-Christian ethic that sin leads to judgment, so it should not surprise us that the early Christians believed that increased persecution upon them signaled an imminent final judgment.

Most in the early church thought Jesus was coming in their lifetimes. Intensifying persecution was a sign that his coming was near. They also believed that judgment would begin with God's people and then extend in ever greater levels of intensity to the ungodly. In a sense the persecution that "goes around" would one day "come around" for the persecutors. To be blunt, heaven awaits the persecuted, and hell awaits the unrepentant persecutors.

I believe that revival often results from having faithfully endured difficult times. I am convinced that the "crushing" effect of persecution has a purifying element. Once we emerge from the storm, our spirits are particularly receptive to God.

A Spiritual Progression Cycle

1. Spiritual Movement.

2. Persecution.

3. Faithful Endurance.

4. Cessation of Persecution.

5. Refined Souls.

6. Collective Revival.

> So if you are suffering in a manner that pleases God, keep on doing what is right, and trust your lives to the God who created you, for he will never fail you.
> (1 Peter 4:19)

When we are going through fires and storms, we need to ask ourselves two questions: are we suffering for righteousness or for shame, and are we dealing with our suffering in a manner that is pleasing to God? If suffering is coming because we are obeying God and we are dealing with it in godly ways, Peter gives us three final pieces of advice: keep, trust, and know.

Final Advice from Peter

Keep on doing what is right.

Trust your life to God.

Know God will never fail you.

If I could have written the script for my life, there would have been no pain, no death, no disappointment, no heartbreak, no suffering, and no persecution. That may have been a 100-percent cotton, crisply pressed, and unwrinkled life, but I can tell you that I would not be the man, the Christian, or the leader I am today without having endured all of those things. It is through the "fire and storm" that God continues to build us, mold us, sculpt us, equip us, teach us, and refine us. I have learned that God is faithful when I get it right, and God is faithful when I get it wrong. He is faithful when my boat floats, and he is faithful when my boat sinks. He is faithful in revival, and he is faithful in persecution. We can trust our lives to God because faithfulness isn't just what God does; it is who God is.

Questions for Discussion and Reflection

1. It is difficult to remain positive during persecution and strife. What are the positives for doing so?

2. Are we suffering for righteousness or for shame and are we dealing with our suffering in a manner that is pleasing to God?

Leading Well (in Troubled Times)

As Peter nears the conclusion of this letter, he appeals to the leadership of the churches. He knows how they handle themselves during these waves of intense persecution will determine much about the future of the church. A steady leader is a steady church. An unhinged leader is an unhinged church. One of the things I have decided over the past few years is that I am not going to publicly debate, "fuss, spit, and fight" with other Christians. I just can't see how social media "holy wars" honor God or bring people to Jesus, but I can clearly see how they erode our witness to the world. I have some friends who consider debate to be their ministry and others who think I should do more of it, but I am not going to do it. What I am going to do is love God and neighbor, invite people to Jesus, stand firm in my convictions, and faithfully preach and teach the Bible. In tumultuous times leaders have to be very intentional because everything they say, write, tweet, or post is being watched closely by someone. Everything they don't say, write, tweet, or post is being watched as well. Peter knows when persecution comes around, it will find the leaders first. I have said this many times over: "The only time it is easy to be a leader is when leadership is not required."

One of the oldest and most effective techniques for shutting down an unwanted movement is to take the primary leader out of play. There are not a lot of true leaders in the world. The good ones greatly inspire those who follow them. Take out the ringleader, and often the air goes out of the movement. People lose heart, and when people lose heart, people go home. There are lots of ways to take leaders out, and history has tried them all. You can bribe them, disenfranchise them, compromise them, extort them, threaten them, jail them, or kill them. It doesn't really matter how you take a leader out, as long as they are no longer leading. However, the riskiest play of all is killing a leader because if they are popular enough and their ideas are strong enough, they will become martyrs, and then you have a real problem. This was the play the temple establishment made on Jesus when all other plays were exhausted. They crucified Jesus hoping his followers would scatter quickly and the whole "Messiah" thing would be over. Instead, Jesus rose from the dead, and other leaders such as Peter, John, and Paul emerged to fill the leadership vacuum. Under the influence of the Holy Spirit, the movement got stronger after Jesus left the earth than it was while he was on the earth.

There is also an element of spiritual warfare to this. Satan will do everything he can to take out effective leaders. If you don't believe me, just step into leadership. It is like walking through the woods during shotgun season wearing a deer suit and an antler hat. Peter knows there is a cultural, political, and spiritual target on leaders that only intensifies during persecution. He addresses the leaders of the churches of Asia Minor directly in this section, not as an apostle, but as a fellow leader.

And now, a word to you who are elders in the churches. I, too, am an elder and a witness to the sufferings of Christ. And I, too, will share in his glory when he is revealed to the whole world. (1 Peter 5:1a)

Elders come out of the Old Testament tradition as the older, wiser, and more respected male leaders in a city. Elders would often sit by the city gates, receive the latest news, and administer the social and religious affairs of their community. They also served as judges concerning civil affairs, screened visitors, were at least morally "devout-ish" in comparison with everyone else (or just too old to get in much trouble), and generally worked to keep harmony within the walls and keep the peace outside them.

In New Testament Judaism, elders became associated with those who led in the Jewish synagogues. Any city in the empire housing at least ten Jewish families was eligible for a synagogue. We know from archeology that there were first-century Jewish synagogues all over the Mediterranean. Archeologists are finding more first-century synagogues all the time. Elders led these Jewish micro-faith communities in regular prayer, Scripture reading, and remembrance of Jewish feasts and traditions. In Jerusalem you had the temple. It was the heart and soul of the Jewish faith. Synagogues were outposts designed to keep Jewish people Jewish.

The moniker of elder was carried to the leaders of the early church. The concept eventually morphed into what we call ordained clergy, people "set apart" to conduct vocational ministry. A huge responsibility of early church planters such as Paul and Barnabas was to choose, equip, ordain, deploy, and supervise the leaders they left in each community once they moved on to the next place. Various texts imply that by this time eldership had shifted from a role to a vocation. As churches grew, church leadership took more time than a secularly employed leader could offer, so people pitched in to compensate them for their time. Elders were increasingly full-time pastors, and some of Peter's, and many of Paul's, instructions address this reality. Though all Christians were called to ministry, elders were ordained to an office, an official position of leadership. Deacons emerged as another office that assisted and supported the elders.

As a fellow elder, I appeal to you. (1 Peter 5:1b)

The appeal of Peter does not come as one "above" those to whom he writes (as Paul's writing sometimes does). It comes as a fellow pastor. The idea is that *"I am one of you. I lead with you. I am targeted like you, and I suffer like you."* No one had to tell anyone that Peter wasn't exactly like any of them since he had been the leader of Jesus' twelve disciples, but this was a humble appeal and one that was sure to be taken well.

Let's take a look at what Peter is asking of the elders in Asia Minor during these troubled times of rampant persecution.

Care for the flock that God has entrusted to you.
(1 Peter 5:2a)

Ancient shepherds led the sheep from the front, whereas herders drove the goats from behind. Peter is consistent with Jewish thinking that godly leadership more resembles shepherding than herding and that faithful followers are far more like sheep than goats. Leaning into pastoral images such as Psalm 23, Peter sets elders as shepherds that God has entrusted to lead his beloved sheep.

Watch over it willingly, not grudgingly—not for what you will get out of it, but because you are eager to serve God. Don't lord it over the people assigned to your care, but lead them by your own good example. (1 Peter 5:2b–3)

This points to six crucial mandates that comprise the job description of elders.

Peter's Charge to Elders

Care for God's people. I often tell prospective church staffers and pastors, "Make sure you are called to this because ministry is too hard to do without a true sense of calling." Ministry is a tough way to make a living. It always has been. Elders should have a clear sense of calling and truly be concerned about the spiritual welfare of the people entrusted to them. If you don't love God's people or want God's very best for them, you shouldn't be an elder, regardless of how gifted you may be.

Don't be a hireling. Hired shepherds worked only for the paycheck. They had a marketable skill set, and they offered it for sale to the highest bidder. They may well have not liked their jobs or may not have even liked sheep, but they had to make a living, so they went to work. But when things got difficult or dangerous, hirelings would simply quit the field. Hirelings were not going to do a single thing they weren't being paid to do.

When I was in late high school and early college, I worked full-time as a security guard at the DuQuoin State Fairgrounds. The fairgrounds was a sprawling enterprise, consisting of surprisingly beautiful abandoned strip mines, and my job was to be there at night to ensure bad things didn't happen. One of my jobs was to walk the expansive interior grandstand area and make sure the office and vendor doors were locked and no intruders were around. One night around 2:00 a.m. I was walking through the grandstand, and I startled an intruder, who started running. I chased the intruder for about ten yards, but as I ran, I was doing some serious thinking. "I am unarmed. The intruder may be armed. What am I going to do with him if I catch this guy? What if I catch him and he stabs me or shoots me? I make four bucks an hour . . ." Do I need to tell you how this story ended? I stopped running. My incident report stated, "2:00 a.m. Intruder in the grandstand. Narrowly escaped. Called the police." I was a hireling.

Peter is reminding elders that if God called you to be a shepherd, you can't quit just because it is dangerous or the sheep are too difficult. You can be released, you can even be fired, but you can't quit.

Lead willingly. One of the things God has given me through all the years of being a pastor is "energy around" and a "mind for" church stuff. I feel called to what I do, I feel gifted for what I do, I feel God put me on earth to do it, and I lead willingly. Is it always easy? No, but I believe if God calls us to a thing and we have a willing spirit, God will supply sustained passion for that thing. If God calls you, don't whine about it.

Lead altruistically. As I mentioned, most elders were probably serving vocationally by this writing, but Peter is adamant that compensation must not be the primary motivation for ministry. Elders must lead because God has called them, the Holy Spirit has equipped them, and they have no other ambition than to be faithful to God and effective in ministry. I tell pastors all the time not to worry about money but to just focus on growing their churches. I have never met a single pastor who was highly effective in a church who didn't get a raise.

Don't be a dictator. Our worship pastor at Christ Church, Don Frazure, studied at the prestigious Juilliard School in New York City. When people around here start bending his ear, I will often joke, "Don, you may have to drop the J-Bomb on them." I don't think he ever has. Peter also had a "J-Bomb": Jesus. If someone was bending his ear about ministry, he could have easily reminded them that he was the head of the disciples. I love that Peter isn't name-dropping or going all "Hollywood." He is trying to spiritually equip leaders for the persecution that is at hand. Peter was trained by the best and most humble leader of all time.

Lead by example. I have known many people who say all the right things, but they cannot live even close to the standard they demand for others. We rightly call this hypocrisy. Hypocrisy is the distance between who we are and who people think us to be. The modern idea is to lower the standard so more people can meet it. That is often called authenticity today, but that was never the Jesus approach. In fact, rather than lowering the bar, Jesus kept raising the bar until it was clear that none of us could leap it except by the power of the Holy Spirit. Good leaders don't just lead with words. They close the hypocrisy gap. The better you know a truly humble and godly leader, the more you will respect them. Good leaders walk the walk and talk the talk with integrity.

And when the Great Shepherd appears, you will receive a crown of never-ending glory and honor. (1 Peter 5:4)

This is a reminder that even excellent shepherds serve under the authority of the Great Shepherd. As hard as shepherding can be, those who serve well will receive an eternal reward.

In Roman culture sports were a big deal. Unlike the modern Olympics where medals are awarded made of precious metals, the victors in ancient athletics received a crown made of organic things such as vines, vegetables, or flowers. Celery was actually a favorite. Regardless, the ancient prizes were perishable, and this is the idea into which Peter is tapping. Peter is resolute that the honor and glory coming to faithful leaders, especially those leading through difficult times, will be eternal, not temporary. Jesus called it "[storing] your treasures in heaven" (Matthew 6:20). A big idea in 1 Peter is, "Not everything we do for God will be rewarded in time and space, but it will be rewarded."

In the same way, you younger men must accept the authority of the elders. And all of you, serve each other in humility, for "God opposes the proud but favors the humble." (1 Peter 5:5)

This is an appeal to order in the church, and again it comes from a position of humility. Peter has told the elders to lead, and he now asks the young men to submit to their wisdom and authority.

A few years ago, Melissa and I heard the legendary bluegrass musician Ricky Skaggs play locally. As great a musician as he is, we discovered that in live performances he is prone to launch into long, and not always riveting, stories. As he was about to settle into "long story number two" that evening, I noticed a couple of the young musicians in his band make eye contact and roll their eyes at each other. My first response was, "You have got to be kidding me. This guy has won fifteen Grammy Awards doing what you all do. When either of the two of you accomplish one one-hundredth of what Skaggs has accomplished, you may be able to wink." And then the spirit of "grouchy old dude" lifted, and it occurred to me that this is what young guys do. I'll bet Ricky Skaggs did it too as a young man when he played with Bill Monroe. And one day those young men will grow out of youthful arrogance, and if they truly become great, young guys will one day roll their eyes at them. That being said, those young guys need to watch out. If Skaggs gets wind of it, he may just fire the whole lot of them. That is what Peter is saying to the young men in the churches. "Your time will come, but that time is not today. So show some respect." Support the elders.

I am very conscious that every opportunity I have been given, every ounce of success I have enjoyed, and every good thing in my life has come to me because of the sacrifice of others. To everyone in his church during these troubled times, Peter asks they "clothe" themselves in humility concerning how they treat one another. Humble people pull together. Humble people get along. Humble people show deep respect. Peter adds that the humble receive God's grace, but God actively stands against the proud. Proud people stand on the wrong side of God.

> So humble yourselves under the mighty power of God, and at the right time he will lift you up in honor.
> (1 Peter 5:6)

I define humility as "confidence rooted in the power of God." Humility is knowing that in my own strength, my lid is low, but if I allow the Holy Spirit to work through me, my ceiling spirals to the cosmos! The Bible verse best depicting my understanding of humility is, "I can do everything through Christ, who gives me strength" (Philippians 4:13). The hack is to minister in the power of the Holy Spirit. Success in our own strength produces pride, and God brings down the proud. Success in the Spirit leads to humility, and God lifts up the humble.

In our previous home, we had a wood-burning fireplace. It was cool, but it was a lot of work. We would open the flue, eventually we would get the split wood started, and the fire would burn until there was no wood left to consume. When the fire went out, there was nothing left but ashes. At the cabin we have a gas-burning fireplace. The fake wood is ornamental because it is gas that fuels the fire, not real wood. Peter argues that if we serve God in our own power during challenging times, we become the fuel source. It should be no wonder so many folks "burn out" when ministry gets tough. But if we serve in the power of God, the Holy Spirit is the fuel, and it comes with unending supply. Only in a spirit of humility can we be like the bush Moses encountered in the desert: burning but not consumed.

The last part of this verse continues the ongoing biblical theme of vindication of the faithful. The faithful get beat up, God rewards the faithful, and the faithless get to watch. If this seems un-Christian to you, you will have to take it up with God because we see this theme over and over. David said it well in Psalm 23:5: "You prepare a table before me in the presence of my enemies" (NIV). Once again, the faithful are vindicated, and the wicked get to watch.

Our final verse today captures my imagination. I have spoken at a gazillion pastor's conferences over the years. I can imagine Peter doing the same here as he addresses his leaders. Indulge me for a moment. In my mind's eye, I can see Peter about to wrap up his final talk at a pastor's conference. Then he asks all the pastors to gather around him. I can see him shift out of teaching gear and into pastoral gear and can easily imagine him grabbing the hands of these elders with compassion in his heart. With love and tears flowing out of him, Peter says . . .

> Give all your worries and cares to God, for he cares about you. (1 Peter 5:7)

The elders to whom Peter spoke had plenty to worry about. Persecution was coming in waves, and Nero was at least "two grapes and a pecan" short of a fruit salad. At any time any one of them could be arrested, beaten, jailed, or martyred. Who would take care of their wives and families if that happened? I assure you that pastors didn't have disability insurance or pensions back then. The temptation was to walk away, deciding this was someone else's fight, and Nero would have let them do just that . . . but they didn't. They remained faithful when it was easy and faithful when it was hard. These courageous elders are being reminded that in the same way they care for their families and congregations, God cares for them.

God cares for you. Can you hear him say, "Give your cares and your worries to me, for I care for you"?

Are you worried about your health? Give it to God.

Are you worried about your finances? Give it to God.

Are you worried about your family? Give it to God.

Are you worried about our country? Give it to God.

Are you worried about our world? Give it to God.

Why can we give God the things about which we most care? Because God cares most about us!

Questions for Discussion and Reflection

1. Write a prayer for your ministry leaders below.

2. Write down your worries below followed by "I give this to God" after each one.

The Prowling Lion

I don't know if you believe in a literal devil, but if you had my job, you would. I am not a guy who sees a demon under every rock, but I do have a pastoral file for "Spiritual Attack." The one thing I have learned over the past thirty-five years of ministry is that if the attack is spiritual in nature, good business practice (even when baptized) won't address it.

Spiritual problems can be addressed only by spiritual solutions.

One of the things I feel called to do is help people anticipate, prepare for, and fend off spiritual attacks. To put it most succinctly, anytime we take new spiritual ground in our lives, we should expect spiritual counterattack. I think the place to start is to learn to identify a spiritual attack and distinguish it from a bad stretch of highway. I have some thoughts.

Discerning Spiritual Attack

Timing. The challenge arrives after you have made significant spiritual movement.

Complexity. This is when practical solutions fail to address simple problems.

Illusive nature. This refers to an inability to nail down root causes. "This shouldn't be such a big deal."

Negative synergy. The situation is more significant than the sum of its parts.

Distraction. Significant energy is being drained from missional things and consumed by non-missional things.

Weakening. The situation results in the neglect of spiritual disciplines and spiritual leadership.

Unholy positioning. People are actively working to "get ahead" at the expense of others or working toward destruction of others. "Even right things seem to be done wrongly."

Non-redemptive. The situation does not lead to personal repentance or reconciliation.

Condemning. This occurs when condemnation is the outcome of the process, rather than conviction that leads to repentance.

Spiritual attacks are wars waged on the battlefields of our minds. They are demonic by nature. The longer the scrap, the more damage that is done. The end result of spiritual attack is to discourage Christians and, if possible, drive them from the faith altogether. Satan employs a scorched-earth policy. If I determine something to be a spiritual attack, here is how I counter-attack.

Responding to Spiritual Warfare

Prayer and fasting. A great question to ask is, "How many actual hours have you spent in prayer about your situation?" Talk less. Pray more.

Identification of strongholds. Literally write down in single words what is going on in your situation (i.e., confusion, gossip, self-pity, ambition, distrust, pride, lust). List these things and get some prayer warriors together to specifically pray against them.

Fasting. How serious are you about this? We fast so God can get our attention, not to get God's attention.

Personal repentance. Repenting of any intentional or unintentional role I may have played in a difficult situation never has a downside.

Calling. Bring things to an end one way or the other. Satan will keep things swirling as long as he can.

Taking authority. There is power in the name of Jesus.

Renewed commitment to the mission. Get back on the mission. Refocus energy from survival to effectiveness. I am far from an expert in spiritual warfare, but I am no novice to the battlefield. I have the scars to prove it. What we take from Satan in this life, we must rip from his hands, and what we rip from his hands, we must hold on to most tightly if we are to retain it. I have become convinced that learning to identify what is (and is not) a spiritual attack and employing a strategy for conducting, and emerging from, spiritual warfare is essential for not only the conduct of ministry but effective Christian living.

Discouragement is a favorite weapon of Satan because of its effectiveness over time. It is a spiritual siege. Discouraged people ultimately get negative, and negativity is always a contagion. The final section of 1 Peter is about spiritual warfare. Satan is using Emperor Nero and ongoing waves of persecution to attack the churches of Asia Minor. Peter is teaching the churches in his sphere how Satan works to combat the work of Christ and is teaching the church how to combat him. We are given a metaphor, advice, context, and a promise. Here is Peter's final advice:

> Stay alert! Watch out for your great enemy, the devil. He prowls around like a roaring lion, looking for someone to devour. (1 Peter 5:8)

The word translated "devil" literally means "accuser." We might also think of ourselves as the accused, God as the judge, and the devil as our accuser. Let's be clear here. Satan wants to destroy your life and destroy your soul. He does not have limited objectives toward you. His aim is total and eternal destruction. We have a sworn enemy. The Bible is clear that Satan is utterly unscrupulous. He is not just a liar but is the "father of lies." The devil is ultimately against all of humanity, but he is particularly against the people of God. Peter calls him the "adversary," he who is against us. Jesus said in John 10:10, "The thief's purpose is to steal and kill and destroy." His strategy is utterly predictable: keep sinners from conversion, keep the converted from discipleship, and discourage disciples so that they abandon the faith. Satan wants to keep God's work from happening in our lives. If God moves anyway, Satan works to contain it. Peter calls him a "roaring lion."

Short-maned Asiatic and huge Barbary lions once roamed Israel. Israel was an overlap of the extreme southern territory of the Asiatic lions and the far northern territory of the African-based Barbary or Atlas lions. The Bible makes about one hundred references to lions and portrays them both positively (i.e. Jesus the Lion of Judah) and negatively, as we see here. In case you are wondering, there are no lions in modern Israel. They became totally extinct during Crusader times, and today only a few hundred Asiatic lions survive in India (which are making a comeback). Barbary lions are long extinct. Lions are rock stars on nature shows, but lions are utterly savage. They kill or starve, and they kill brutally. We also know that desert lions tended to hunt alone rather than in prides, giving additional clarity to this passage. This makes sense since deserts don't offer much natural cover and desert prey are generally smaller, which doesn't require teamwork. Just as a solitary hungry lion goes on the prowl looking for prey, Satan prowls looking to devour Christians. Lions look for the very young, the very old, the injured, the indecisive, the foolish, and the most vulnerable. Satan hunts in much the same way. In this metaphor Satan is the predator and we are the prey, and we do well to remain vigilant. To quote my high school football coach, "Keep your knees bent, your butt down, and your head up." We also know that starving lions, as well as dogs, boars, and bears, were used in the Roman Colosseum in Nero's reign to kill persecuted Christians for public entertainment. It appears Peter's use of lions was both metaphorical and literal.

Stand firm against him and be strong in your faith. Remember that your family of believers all over the world is going through the same kind of suffering you are. (1 Peter 5:9)

When our church has faced growing pains and spiritual attacks over the years, talking with pastors who had led their churches through such challenges in their own congregations has been invaluable for me. If nothing else, it reminded me that what we were living through was common to churches of our size and stage. Frankly, it was comforting to know we weren't the only ones struggling. Now we move to Peter's instruction to those facing the lion.

Peter's Instruction

Stand firm. Don't back off, give in, or back down.

Be strong. Summon strength from within (spiritual, physical, and mental).

Remember. You are not alone.

When Melissa and I turned into avid hikers in the Smoky Mountains in the early 2000s, one of the first lessons we received was what to do in case of a bear attack. Let's face it: black bears are not overly ferocious creatures, but if you surprise one or meet a mother with cubs who feels threatened, things can go bad quickly. There is another problem with bears. They can outrun you, out-climb you, out-swim you, and out-fight you. If you have to go toe to toe unarmed with a bear, you will never have the better hand. You are going to have to bluff. The idea is to stand your ground and generally take authority over the bear by yelling, waving your hands, and being generally threatening toward it. I have no idea if this works or not. I hope I never find out. But I do know you would be foolish to go into bear country without a plan for combating a potential attack, and that is Peter's point. In our own strength, we are no match for the devil. He can outrun us, out-climb us, out-swim us, and out-fight us. Satan does not back down to us. We don't scare him a bit. But if we will stand our ground and take authority over him, Satan will back down to the Christ who dwells in us. Jesus gives the devil nightmares eight days a week, and we can take authority over Satan in the name of Jesus.

> In his kindness God called you to share in his eternal glory by means of Christ Jesus. (1 Peter 5:10a)

The saving gospel of Christ is brought to us by the kindness and favor of God toward us. Salvation is not a prize to be earned; it is a gift to be received. God wanted us, sin separates us, Jesus bridged the gap, and by accepting Christ, our eternal future is secured.

> So after you have suffered a little while, he will restore, support, and strengthen you, and he will place you on a firm foundation. (1 Peter 5:10b–11)

The Bible teaches that tough times don't last forever. God wins. Like storms at sea, persecution can be survived. The weather is almost always good immediately after a storm. If we hold course and weather our storms, we receive four promises from God.

Post-Storm Promises

God will restore us. The Greek word here means to fix or to mend. The idea is that surviving periods of suffering has a re-parative quality upon our character. In Christ we will emerge from bad times as better people than when we entered them. What was taken from us is restored, and what is weak within us is strengthened. We get back what Satan steals and more. **God will support us.** This can equally be translated as "establish." The connotation is that we will emerge from suffering ever more solidified in our faith.

God will strengthen us. If difficult times weaken us in the short term, God promises to renew us with strength on the other side. Isaiah was getting at this when he wrote, "Those who hope in the Lord will renew their strength" (Isaiah 40:31, NIV).

God will set us in a secure place. My translation of this concept would be to deepen our footers. The ancients built incredible structures, but an earthquake could topple a whole city. They didn't seem to understand that you have to dig deep to survive turbulent times. Persecution deepens our roots and solidifies our foundations.

Peter reminds his churches that not only will God get us through the storms, but he will repair the storm damage, make us strong as granite, renew our strength, and lay our foundations deep. We come out better on the other side.

All power to him forever! Amen. (1 Peter 5:11)

I love this tendency in Peter! The Gospels present young Peter as a highly excitable and impulsive guy with "foot-in-mouth disease." No one gets it more right or wrong than Peter. Clearly, he matures into a more measured leader by this writing, but there are times Peter still gets so caught up in his own preaching that he starts shouting, "Amen!" This is one of them!

Over the past three years, our church has endured a sharply divided nation, cultural wars, debates over human sexuality, a contentious presidential election, a global pandemic, intense mitigation divides, and a denominational disaffiliation. Not only have we survived, but we have come out more holy and united. We are better focused, stronger, and deeper than we would have ever been otherwise. We navigated the course, held steady, stayed faithful to God's Word, refused to succumb to fear, kept on loving each other, and stayed on mission. If Peter were here right now, he would look at us and say, "Amen! See, I told you this would happen!"

 ## Questions for Discussion and Reflection

1. Have you ever faced a time of spiritual warfare? How did you know it was spiritual in nature?

2. Are you going through a difficult time? Search for and write down Scriptures that can restore, support, strengthen, and secure you in the storms.

STANDING FIRM IN GRACE

One of the core values of my life is to invest in the spiritual development of my grandchildren. Since I live thirty minutes from them and they are all busy, this time has to be intentional. Whether we are playing baseball, chatting in a text, visiting at the cabin, or having a meal somewhere, I pick my spots to speak into their lives. I think most about the "last thing I am going to say" at any given encounter. I want this "last thing" to carry the weight of our entire time together, and I want to give them something of potential impact. It may be a word of encouragement if they are on a rough stretch, something to build character, an assurance of my love for them, or some practical or spiritual advice, but the last thing is always the main thing.

Peter is about to sign off his letter to the persecuted churches of Asia Minor. His humility and pastoral heart have been front and center throughout the entire book. He has now either said all he has to say or said all they can hear, so the letter is about over.

Often this is when people stop reading and expect the Complimentary Close to fade like a bad Western, but I think Peter's final navigation instructions are important to his readers . . . and to us. They are the last thing he is going to say in this letter and, for all he knows, the last thing he will ever say.

> I have written and sent this short letter to you with the help of Silas, whom I commend to you as a faithful brother. (1 Peter 5:12a)

One of the historical challenges to Peter's authorship is the excellence of the refined Greek manuscript. Whoever wrote this letter clearly had a command of the written language that could not possibly be expected from a Galilean fisherman like Peter. This single verse solves this problem. Silas wrote down what Peter spoke and then cleaned it all up into polished literary form. This was not uncommon.

When I travel internationally, I am often asked if I speak a certain language, and I jokingly reply, "I am an American, I speak one language, and I speak it poorly." Americans who have lived in this country for several generations like my family often consider speaking, reading, and writing in English to be bundled together, but for multilingual people, that is not always a correct assumption.

When we are in Israel for our bi-annual pilgrimages, our tour guides always speak English, Arabic, and Hebrew as a baseline, but that does not mean they can write or even read in all of those languages. This would also be true of mid-first-century Jewish Christians across the empire. These folks may well have spoken a regional language or two in addition to Arabic, which was spoken among Jews, and they would have written in Greek. And did I mention Hebrew was an ancestral language? Silas was a Jewish Roman citizen, meaning he would have been well educated, connected, and enfranchised. Buying a Roman citizenship was not cheap. Silas would have enjoyed an education that Peter could not possibly have accessed, and in many ways he is as much translating between two languages as he is taking dictation.

I find Silas a most interesting study. He is a mainstay in the New Testament but is almost always in the "second" chair, despite having a resume that would indicate he checked all the boxes and possessed all the tools needed by a top-tier leader. After Paul and Barnabus broke up their missionary team, Paul chose Silas as his ministry partner. Silas strikes me as a courageous, gifted, and Spirit-filled leader who doesn't have to be in charge of everything or get the credit for everything. His reward is the effectiveness of the early Christian movement. He reminds me of an athlete who chose to contribute to a championship team, rather than be the best player on a mediocre team. For Silas, it is never about himself; it is about the great cause of Jesus Christ! No wonder Peter offers his highest recommendation!

> My purpose in writing is to encourage you and assure you that what you are experiencing is truly part of God's grace for you. (1 Peter 5:12b)

When we go through difficult times and suffer for our faith, it is good to receive encouragement. People who care in our darkest hours remind us that God cares. We have all experienced the lifting power of the right word said at the right time by the right person. Sometimes just hearing, "It's going to be alright" can go a long way, but it is the second part of this verse that intrigues me. Peter is assuring his persecuted followers they are walking in "God's grace." He claims their sufferings past, present, and future are clear evidence of the "grace" or "favor" of God, not the punishment or disfavor of God.

Some years back a leader in our church called it quits. I was saddened but not surprised. We were on a tough stretch of leadership highway. There were tough decisions to be made, and there were not going to be immediate wins for anyone. I was traveling somewhere and spoke with him on the phone concerning his frustrations one late afternoon. I will never forget his words: "Leading a church shouldn't be this hard." His assumption was that if we are hearing God, things should not be difficult. Peter is assuring his readers that nothing could be further from the truth. Furthermore, the Christians in Asia Minor were presently enduring hardship precisely because they were in God's will. Their hardships would prove to make them all the more fit for God's service in this life and for eternal glory in the life to come.

Stand firm in this grace. (1 Peter 5:12c)

Were I to point to a single message from 1 Peter, it would be to "stand firm." I spent a lot of 2019, 2020, and 2021 standing firm in the historic Christian faith—not radiating at a high frequency and not mad at anyone but not backing down either. God's call to our church was to "stand firm in grace." I believe God has rewarded that stance.

There are four assumptions being made when we say, "Stand firm in this grace . . ."

Standing Firm in Grace

We know the faith. Persecution forces us to examine the foundations of our faith and clarify our understandings of the faith.

We must accept the faith. Persecution makes us ask, "Do we still believe this stuff, even if it costs us more than we ever imagined?" You can stand firm only with an owned faith; a rented one just won't do.

We must not waver in the faith. Persecution tests the structural integrity of our beliefs. I believe in the power of single-mindedness. I tell people all the time, "You just have to make up your mind because until you do, you are just going to get blown all over the place." When it comes to faith, we must "know that we know that we know."

We must know God will reward the faithful. The New Testament is consistent in teaching that the faithful will be rewarded. We can hang tough in the worst of times because we believe God is faithful.

> Your sister church here in Babylon sends you greetings, and so does my son Mark. (1 Peter 5:13)

I believe the use of the word "Babylon" here is metaphorical and refers to Rome, in part because the orientation of the New Testament world is west (the Mediterranean), rather than east (like the Old Testament), and in part because the embodiment of evil had metaphorically shifted from Nebuchadnezzar and Babylon in the Old Testament to Caesar and Rome in the New Testament. We also know Peter is associated with Rome in tradition, so I think it likely that he writes from there.

Mark is most probably John Mark, the writer of Mark's Gospel. He was the point of contention between Paul and Barnabas when he abandoned the First Missionary Journey in 45 AD as a very young man. Barnabas wanted to give John

Mark another chance. Paul would have nothing of it. He couldn't afford the risk. One of the things the Bible makes clear is that Mark later redeemed himself after his failure in the eyes of everyone . . . even Paul. Perhaps Peter, who denied Christ in the courtyard of the high priest so long ago, could relate to John Mark. John Mark is a story of redemption and a story of a second chance actually working out. John Mark is a testimony to the God of second chances. This gives us hope, not just for others but for ourselves.

Greet each other with a kiss of love. (1 Peter 5:14a)

This was a common platonic greeting that was associated with the early church and later seemed to be abandoned because people on the outside misinterpreted it. What has been retained from this practice is the "passing of the peace" in a traditional Christian worship service. This has stuck around and can be as formal as saying, "Peace be with you," which is countered by, "And also with you" or as informal as a greeting time in a worship service. That being said, a few weeks back in church, a couple was sitting behind me during the greeting time. I turned to say hello, but the two were already in the process of giving each other a quick kiss. Somewhat embarrassed when they saw me looking at them, I smiled and said, "I am just going to shake your hands." I did. But their greeting to each other was the biblical one.

Peace be with all of you who are in Christ.
(1 Peter 5:14b)

Peace is the deepest hope of Peter for the beloved people comprising the churches to whom he writes. Certainly, peace is our heart's desire for all we love, especially those who may be caught up in difficult times. But this is more than an "end of a letter platitude." When we experience times of discontinuity, we often pray for peace with the hope that God will bring cessation to the conflict troubling us. The problem is that in a fallen world, that kind of peace seldom arrives, and if it does, it never stays for very long. But if we define peace as "the presence of Christ in the midst of our conflict," peace becomes something very much available to us.

My office has no exterior windows. It is always dark when I walk into work. I have no idea how to extract darkness, but that particular set of skills is not necessary. All I have to do is flip on the light switch, and the lights dispel the darkness. If we think of turmoil as the darkness in a room and Jesus as the light, we lean into Peter's understanding of peace. Just turn on the light. Where Jesus is, there is peace.

Questions for Discussion and Reflection

1. Do you need encouragement? Write a prayer expressing how you feel and asking God for encouragement.

2. What are some of your biggest takeaways from 1 Peter?

THE END OF OUR TRAIL

We have now come to the end of our journey through 1 Peter.
If we view this last segment of his letter as summative, this is
the "last word" Peter leaves to us as we navigate forward.

Six Closing Thoughts from Peter

1. **Kudos to "behind the scenes" people.** As a person
   who has spent his career on the stage, I am forever in
   debt to those behind the scenes. I am so grateful for
   each person who faithfully serves without the spot-
   light or the notoriety of being up front. Shout out to
   every Silas of the world who adds value to every team
   and makes every leader even better. Let's sing a song
   to the unsung heroes of every church, every family,
   and every office. You are not forgotten by God.

2. **If you are walking in Christ in a difficult time,
   be encouraged.** Persecution and pushback do not
   necessarily mean you are doing something wrong.
   They mean you are doing something. Be encouraged
   that you are gifted by the Holy Spirit and being used
   by God as a catalyst for the Kingdom. Consider it an
   honor that Satan is so concerned about your impact
   for God that he is countering you directly. Those who
   are faithful in the hard times are those who will be
   faithful at all times.

3. **Stand firm in assurance that God's promises are faithful.** I grew up with the axiom of "God said it, I believe it, and it is so." I still like it. Because God's promises are faithful, we don't have to worry. I had a buddy in high school named Donny who was always late. Anytime he was supposed to pick you up to go anywhere or do anything was a "give or take" four hours. There was one occasion when he was going to pick me up to go somewhere one Friday night. He showed up about an hour before the time he gave me . . . on Saturday. He casually responded, "Sorry I was late." Donny was intrinsically unreliable, and if you were counting on him, you were doomed before you started. God is the opposite of that. His promises are fulfilled, and they are fulfilled right on time.

4. **Celebrate the God of second chances.** Sometimes giving people a second chance blows up in your face, perhaps even more often than not. But sometimes it doesn't, and that changes everything. Barnabas gave John Mark another chance on the missionary front when Paul would not, and Peter is the beneficiary of Barnabas' risk. We don't just give people a second chance for ourselves. We give it for others as well. Some of you are the evidence of the redemptive power of the second chance . . . and beyond. One reason to not give up on others is because God has not given up on you. We wouldn't have the Gospel of Mark apart from John Mark getting a second chance.

5. **Have warm hearts toward one another.** In difficult and challenging times, we must maintain genuine affection toward each other. Jesus said the defining characteristic of his followers should be our love for each other. The difference between a good team and a great team is how well they perform under pressure.

Great teams refuse to stop believing in themselves, collapse, and turn against one another. They keep on executing their plays despite hardship because they believe in what they are doing and they believe in each other. Adversity that will break a good team will make a great team, and persecution that will break a good church will make another church great. It is relational equity that gets us through tough times. This equity exists on both a horizontal (relationships with each other) and a vertical (relationship with God) axis.

6. **Invite the presence of Christ into your trouble.** We end with a prayer technique for those immersed in the storm. Invite Jesus into the midst of what you are going through and know that where Jesus is, there is peace. "Jesus be present in my sick body, my troubled mind, my fractured emotions, and my doubting spirit" is always a prayer God wants to answer, and the answer is not found in the solution or resolution. It is found in Christ himself.

When Peter's audience had this letter publicly read to them, they had to experience a feeling of being both heard and encouraged. Peter "got" them and their situation. He cared deeply. Peter's readers also left realizing that as bad as things were, they would soon get even worse. Not every difficult thing we face in a fallen world gets better. As ever intensifying persecution continues to pound the churches of Asia Minor, Peter will soon feel compelled to write a follow-up letter to provide even more instruction, warning, and encouragement as events unfold. This letter will be less pastoral and more intense. It will be our next trail we will traverse together.

Thank you for the opportunity to guide you through 1 Peter. It is an honor I will never take for granted.